NoLey 11|12

PEACHTREE CITY
PLAN TO STAY™

AIMEE SEMPLE McPHERSON

SPIRITUAL LEADERS AND THINKERS

MARY BAKER EDDY

MOHANDAS GANDHI

AYATOLLAH RUHOLLAH KHOMEINI

MARTIN LUTHER

AIMEE SEMPLE McPHERSON

THOMAS MERTON

DALAI LAMA (TENZIN GYATSO)

SPIRITUAL
LEADERS AND
THINKERS

AIMEE SEMPLE McPHERSON

Silvia Anne Sheafer

Introductory Essay by
Martin E. Marty, Professor Emeritus
University of Chicago Divinity School

CHELSEA HOUSE
PUBLISHERS
A Haights Cross Communications Company
Philadelphia

CHELSEA HOUSE PUBLISHERS

VP, New Product Development Sally Cheney
Director of Production Kim Shinners
Creative Manager Takeshi Takahashi
Manufacturing Manager Diann Grasse

Staff for AIMEE SEMPLE McPHERSON

Executive Editor Lee Marcott
Senior Editor Tara Koellhoffer
Production Editor Megan Emery
Assistant Photo Editor Noelle Nardone
Series and Cover Designer Keith Trego
Layout 21st Century Publishing and Communications, Inc.

A Haights Cross Communications ◢◤ Company

www.chelseahouse.com

First Printing

9 8 7 6 5 4 3 2 1

Library of Congress Cataloging-in-Publication Data applied for.

ISBN 0-7910-7867-1

CONTENTS

Foreword

Why become acquainted with notable people when making efforts to understand the religions of the world?

Most of the faith communities number hundreds of millions of people. What can attention paid to one tell about more, if not most, to say nothing of *all*, their adherents? Here is why:

The people in this series are exemplars. If you permit me to take a little detour through medieval dictionaries, their role will become clear.

In medieval lexicons, the word *exemplum* regularly showed up with a peculiar definition. No one needs to know Latin to see that it relates to "example" and "exemplary." But back then, *exemplum* could mean something very special.

That "ex-" at the beginning of such words signals "taking out" or "cutting out" something or other. Think of to "excise" something, which is to snip it out. So, in the more interesting dictionaries, an *exemplum* was referred to as "a clearing in the woods," something cut out of the forests.

These religious figures are *exempla*, figurative clearings in the woods of life. These clearings and these people perform three functions:

First, they define. You can be lost in the darkness, walking under the leafy canopy, above the undergrowth, plotless in the pathless forest. Then you come to a clearing. It defines with a sharp line: there, the woods end; here, the open space begins.

Great religious figures are often stumblers in the dark woods.

We see them emerging in the bright light of the clearing, blinking, admitting that they had often been lost in the mysteries of existence, tangled up with the questions that plague us all, wandering without definition. Then they discover the clearing, and, having done so, they point our way to it. We then learn more of who we are and where we are. Then we can set our own direction.

Second, the *exemplum*, the clearing in the woods of life, makes possible a brighter vision. Great religious pioneers in every case experience illumination and then they reflect their light into the hearts and minds of others. In Buddhism, a key word is *enlightenment*. In the Bible, "the people who walked in darkness have seen a great light." They see it because their prophets or savior brought them to the sun in the clearing.

Finally, when you picture a clearing in the woods, an *exemplum*, you are likely to see it as a place of cultivation. Whether in the Black Forest of Germany, on the American frontier, or in the rain forests of Brazil, the clearing is the place where, with light and civilization, residents can cultivate, can produce culture. As an American moviegoer, my mind's eye remembers cinematic scenes of frontier days and places that pioneers hacked out of the woods. There, they removed stones, planted, built a cabin, made love and produced families, smoked their meat, hung out laundered clothes, and read books. All that can happen in clearings.

In the case of these religious figures, planting and cultivating and harvesting are tasks in which they set an example and then inspire or ask us to follow. Most of us would not have the faintest idea how to find or be found by God, to nurture the Holy Spirit, to create a philosophy of life without guidance. It is not likely that most of us would be satisfied with our search if we only consulted books of dogma or philosophy, though such may come to have their place in the clearing.

Philosopher Søren Kierkegaard properly pointed out that you cannot learn to swim by being suspended from the ceiling on a belt and reading a "How To" book on swimming. You learn because a parent or an instructor plunges you into water, supports you when necessary, teaches you breathing and motion, and then releases you to swim on your own.

Kierkegaard was not criticizing the use of books. I certainly have nothing against books. If I did, I would not be commending this series to you, as I am doing here. For guidance and courage in the spiritual quest, or—and this is by no means unimportant!—in intellectual pursuits, involving efforts to understand the paths others have taken, there seems to be no better way than to follow a fellow mortal, but a man or woman of genius, depth, and daring. We "see" them through books like these.

Exemplars come in very different styles and forms. They bring differing kinds of illumination, and then suggest or describe diverse patterns of action to those who join them. In the case of the present series, it is possible for someone to repudiate or disagree with *all* the religious leaders in this series. It is possible also to be nonreligious and antireligious and therefore to disregard the truth claims of all of them. It is more difficult, however, to ignore them. Atheists, agnostics, adherents, believers, and fanatics alike live in cultures that are different for the presence of these people. "Leaders and thinkers" they may be, but most of us do best to appraise their thought in the context of the lives they lead or have led.

If it is possible to reject them all, it is impossible to affirm everything that all of them were about. They disagree with each other, often in basic ways. Sometimes they develop their positions and ways of thinking by separating themselves from all the others. If they met each other, they would likely judge each other cruelly. Yet the lives of each and all of them make a contribution to the intellectual and spiritual quests of those who go in ways other than theirs. There are tens of thousands of religions in the world, and millions of faith communities. Every one of them has been shaped by founders and interpreters, agents of change and prophets of doom or promise. It may seem arbitrary to walk down a bookshelf and let a finger fall on one or another, almost accidentally. This series may certainly look arbitrary in this way. Why precisely the choice of these exemplars?

In some cases, it is clear that the publishers have chosen someone who has a constituency. Many of the world's 54 million Lutherans may be curious about where they got their name, who the man Martin Luther was. Others are members of a community but choose isolation: The hermit monk Thomas Merton is typical. Still others are exiled and achieve their work far from the clearing in which they grew up; here the Dalai Lama is representative. Quite a number of the selected leaders had been made unwelcome, or felt unwelcome in the clearings, in their own childhoods and youth. This reality has almost always been the case with women like Mary Baker Eddy or Aimee Semple McPherson. Some are extremely controversial: Ayatollah Ruhollah Khomeini stands out. Yet to read of this life and thought as one can in this series will be illuminating in much of the world of conflict today.

Reading of religious leaders can be a defensive act: Study the lives of certain ones among them and you can ward off spiritual— and sometimes even militant—assaults by people who follow them. Reading and learning can be a personally positive act: Most of these figures led lives that we can indeed call exemplary. Such lives can throw light on communities of people who are in no way tempted to follow them. I am not likely to be drawn to the hermit life, will not give up my allegiance to medical doctors, or be successfully nonviolent. Yet Thomas Merton reaches me and many non-Catholics in our communities; Mary Baker Eddy reminds others that there are more ways than one to approach healing; Mohandas Gandhi stings the conscience of people in cultures like ours where resorting to violence is too frequent, too easy.

Finally, reading these lives tells something about how history is made by imperfect beings. None of these subjects is a god, though some of them claimed that they had special access to the divine, or that they were like windows that provided for illumination to that which is eternal. Most of their stories began with inauspicious childhoods. Sometimes they were victimized, by parents or by leaders of religions from which they later broke.

Some of them were unpleasant and abrasive. They could be ungracious toward those who were near them and impatient with laggards. If their lives were symbolic clearings, places for light, many of them also knew clouds and shadows and the fall of night. How they met the challenges of life and led others to face them is central to the plot of all of them.

I have often used a rather unexciting concept to describe what I look for in books: *interestingness*. The authors of these books, one might say, had it easy, because the characters they treat are themselves so interesting. But the authors also had to be interesting and responsible. If, as they wrote, they would have dulled the personalities of their bright characters, that would have been a flaw as marring as if they had treated their subjects without combining fairness and criticism, affection and distance. To my eye, and I hope in yours, they take us to spiritual and intellectual clearings that are so needed in our dark times.

Martin E. Marty
The University of Chicago

1

China Bound

*It's the hand of God touched my life
and blessed me . . . with the chance to
bring to these people the Gospel.*

—Robert Semple to his wife, Aimee

In June 1910, the *Empress of Ireland* steamed into Hong Kong. Twenty-year-old Aimee Semple and her husband, Robert, stood at the ship's rail awed by the activity in Kowloon Harbor. China, with its millions of people, had long offered a challenge to Christianity. The Semples, young and eager evangelists, were ready to pick up the chalice.

As the steamer slowly plied the dark and deep waters toward its dock, it passed Chinese fishing junks with bright golden winglike sails. The Semples also spotted a red, white, and blue Union Jack flag fluttering above a British warship anchored near an American Navy gunboat. "My heart was young and gay," Aimee Semple later wrote.[1] Sun-tanned sailors in crisp white uniforms waved at the steamer's passengers. "It's—isn't it so *alive*, so *exciting!*" she said.[2] This atmosphere was very different from her home in the farming community of Ingersoll, Canada.

Rolling effortlessly in the swells of the larger crafts were hundreds of sampans that looked like skiffs with woven canopies and a single sail. They were homes to entire families. Under a sunbaked blue sky, puffs of smoke swirled lazily from stacks of ships of French, Spanish, and Italian registry. Tourists, missionaries, and buyers of China's commercial goods looked favorably upon the strange and bountiful Orient.

On the dock, bareback coolies in baggy trousers haggled for fares. Long bamboo poles, with baskets on either end, stretched across their bent shoulders. Other local laborers pulled rickshaws. Chinese mandarins in purple silk robes and soft-soled slippers ignored the outstretched palms of beggars and opium addicts. Even the odors of Hong Kong were distinctive—the aroma of Chinese spices, garlic, and dark soy sauce competed with the stench of decaying garbage and human excretion.

Captivated by the scene before her eyes, Aimee Semple, who was six months pregnant at the time, recalled thinking, "I'm going to adore China."[3] Back home, she had daydreamed of how she would preach. She had once told her husband, "Since I was just a little girl I've felt . . . I know now what I felt all along was God's assurance that He would call me to *serve* Him and win souls for Him."[4] Like the missionaries who had gone before her, Aimee's dedication to God, to the job of saving souls for Jesus, and to preaching the Gospel had no limit.

Christianity first came to China in A.D. 635 in the form of Nestorianism. Unlike today's Christian beliefs, Nestorianism maintained that, in Jesus Christ, a divine being and a human person were joined in perfect harmony in action but not in unity. Bishop Alopen of Persia, who introduced this form of Christianity, declared that Mary was not the Mother of God but the Mother of Christ. When the Portuguese and Spanish Jesuits arrived in the late sixteenth century, they introduced Catholicism to the Ming Dynasty. American missionaries came in the late 1800s. It appears that religious leaders were fervent in their efforts to convert the so-called heathen Chinese to Christianity. Although Chinese Christians were few compared to the country's total population of millions, they made an impact on foreign culture, so much so that non-Christian Chinese periodically waged wars and committed brutalities against native converts and their Christian clerics. Despite the many problems that faced foreign missionaries, though, they continued to believe it was their Christian duty to bring their ministry to Asia.

Aimee and Robert Semple arrived ten years after the defiant Boxers, a group of Chinese nationalists, had slaughtered scores of missionaries and Chinese converts in 1900. In 1911, a year after the Semples' arrival, Sun Yat-sen, the son of a Christian farmer, would return from exile and overthrow the Manchu Dynasty in a revolution.

When Aimee married Robert Semple, an ordained Pentecostal preacher, he told her that he planned to go to China: "China, with her mighty millions offering a continual challenge to Christianity. And here—this busy little island of Macao—this is my destination and point of attack."[5] So intent was he upon his mission that Robert Semple often sang a parody he had made up to the tune of the hymn "Bringing in the Sheaves": "Bringing in the Chinese, bringing in the Chinese, we will come rejoicing bringing in the Chinese." He also faithfully read, and carried with him, the tattered and marked pages of *Pilgrim's Progress*. This allegory written by John Bunyan described the journey of a man named Christian through life to the Celestial City. Christian traveled far and wide to a range of places, and he met a number of symbolic figures. Besides the Bible, this thick, illustrated volume was often the only book that American pioneer families owned.

If internal violence, disease, and periodic famines were not enough of an obstacle to missionaries, then money might be. The missionaries' only source of income came from donations. Although the Pentecostals sent out missionaries, there was no central organization behind them that would help fund a foreign mission. The Semples left Southampton, England, with a total of sixty-five dollars. Like their fellow Christian evangelists, they believed God would provide for their mission. As Robert Semple explained, "Someone will come up and place the money in [my] hands before the gangplank is pulled up." [6]

The Semples' long journey from Southampton was plagued by high winds, a typhoon, and seasickness. Robert kept to his bunk most of the time. Aimee fared better—navigating the tilting deck and eating in the ship's dining room. The Semples' dockside greeting was far more enjoyable than the storms and tropical weather they had endured at sea. On the congested dock was a group of missionaries—men dressed in white suits and sun helmets, and women wearing ankle-length cotton dresses and carrying white parasols lined in green cloth. Though they were of mixed denominations, all of the experienced missionaries were eager to greet the new arrivals. Living thousands of miles from home during a time when telephones were not very common and e-mail was many decades away, they were excited to hear any news the Semples might have to offer. They probably asked about conditions back home and if the Semples had any messages from loved ones.

After a short stay at a local mission house, Robert began preaching with a Chinese interpreter. Aimee went house hunting and eventually found an apartment next to a Hindu temple and down the street from the Happy Valley Cemetery. From her new home, Aimee Semple could hear strange conversations in foreign tongues and eerie, ghostlike moaning. Rats and centipedes haunted the apartment. Funeral processions on their way to the cemetery were frequent. There were military burials with bagpipes and drum and bugle corps; clanging brass bells, banners, and trays of fruits and meats signaled the Chinese interments. Perhaps the saddest sights were the missionary funerals that passed by the Semples' window—small coffins holding the bodies of children who had proven too fragile to survive foreign diseases and the extreme climate of a strange land. Still, these gloomy occurrences were not enough to frighten Aimee—until the Hindus burned one of their own.

One morning, outside her window, black-bearded men in woven turbans and long robes built a pyre for a cremation. A pile of wood was placed on the ground and then the body of the deceased was wrapped in cloth and more wood piled over it. Kerosene was poured on the pyre and then set aflame. Never having witnessed anything like this, Aimee was horrified to see the body draw up its knees as if it were alive. Her screams brought her husband, who comforted her, explaining that the body was moving because the bones and muscles were reacting to the intense heat.

The full impact of the Semples' China mission was personified by Aimee's Cantonese teacher. To preach and to be able to communicate with their congregation, the Semples took language lessons. Aimee Semple asked her teacher if he was a Christian. He shrugged, saying he was not, and she noticed that he seemed bitter about the question. When asked why, his response was illuminating: "You Christians came to China in ships, and at the point of the cannon forced opium and Bibles upon us from the same vessels. Chinese never forget."[7]

During the first summer the Semples spent in Hong Kong, the heat was merciless, often over 100°F. Seeking relief, Aimee went to the cemetery. There, she would lie on the grass amid the tombstones under the comforting shade provided by the leaves of the magnolia trees. By this time, her initially positive feelings about China were changing. "I knew I would never live though the ordeal," she later wrote.[8] Somehow she did survive, but she fell terribly ill with tropical malaria.

For an entire month, she lay under mosquito netting and suffered the agony of variably hot to freezing body temperatures. She worried about the baby she carried and ultimately worried for her husband, who was suffering at the same time with dysentery. Hoping to find a reprieve in a milder climate, the Semples journeyed to the island of Macao, several hours from Hong Kong by ship. Despite the change, Robert Semple's condition grew worse. His wife called for a nurse and doctor to take them back to Hong Kong. Robert Semple was carried to the steamer on a hammock suspended on two bamboo poles, slung between the shoulders of two natives.

The Semples were taken to Matilda Hospital—a mission hospital for the poor. When doctors asked Aimee what she had been feeding her husband, she told them that someone had told her he should have a light diet—a diet of fresh produce. No one had explained that field vegetables were fertilized with human excrement.

While Aimee Semple lay in the women's ward, trying to regain her health and ensure the safety of her unborn child, her husband lay dying in the men's ward. Two months after their arrival in China, he died of dysentery. Fearful that there was no money to bury him, Aimee reportedly told the nurses that she had only five dollars and thirty cents. Then a miracle occurred.

Weeks before, in Chicago, two women said they heard a voice tell them that Aimee was in trouble. They immediately sent sixty dollars to China to help her. This money arrived on the very day that Robert Semple died.

Overcome with grief, Aimee watched from her hospital window as her husband's body was carried by inside a canvas bundle. He was buried in the Happy Valley Cemetery, where they had reposed under the shaded trees. Aimee was too sick to attend the funeral. Robert Semple's service was conducted by fellow missionaries.

Grieving, homesick, and still ill herself, Aimee remained in the hospital until her baby arrived. On September 17, 1910, Roberta Star Semple was born, weighing in at four and a half pounds. For six weeks, Aimee Semple was unable to decide whether she should stay in China and evangelize as her husband had wanted to do or return home. She prayed and asked her late husband for advice. He did not answer. When she was well enough, she cradled Roberta in her arms and went to Happy Valley Cemetery. There, she asked Robert again whether she should she stay in China and preach the Gospel or go home. There was no response. According to Aimee's autobiography, just then, a bird of paradise settled in a nearby tree and Roberta began to cry. Aimee believed she had the answer. Her first duty was to care for her baby—which meant a return to a healthier environment.

Only three months after she had first arrived with her husband, Aimee once again boarded the *Empress of Ireland*, this time alone with her baby. As the ship pulled away from Hong Kong, Aimee stood on deck cradling her daughter. She waved sadly to the courageous souls who had first met her and Robert at the dock. Then she looked out to sea. It seemed, she recalled, that half of her heart was being left behind in the purple shadows of Happy Valley.

2

Growing up

I want to know God! I hunger to know him!
—Aimee Semple McPherson

R ural activities in Salford, Ontario, Canada, in the late 1800s, centered around the changing seasons and the Protestant work ethic, which assured people that if they worked hard they would succeed. In late summer, the rolling fields of wheat and hay glistened golden under a clear sky and warm sunshine. The fertile smell of cattle, pig, and sheep manure drifted over apple and pear orchards, encouraging next year's abundant crops. Nearby Ingersoll was famous for its cheese factory, and local dairy farmers benefited from its reputation as Canada's oldest. In the growing towns of Ingersoll and Salford, Baptist, Methodist, and Presbyterian churches flourished and provided religious guidance for the faithful. The Salvation Army ministry was present, too. Despite some people's distaste for the Army's martial and lively meetings, the more traditional Christian churches rented the organization rooms and halls in which to hold its evangelical programs of repentance and salvation. The fact that the Army raised funds to feed and clothe the poor gave it respectful credibility, if not equal standing as a legitimate religion.

In one of the Salford's more prosperous farmhouses, a young woman awaited the arrival of a baby. Minnie Kennedy, nineteen, was certain that the baby she was carrying was a girl. When Minnie was a child, she had read the biblical story of Hannah and her son, Samuel, whose birth was foretold to his parents by an angel of God. In the story, Hannah was married to Elkanah but was very distressed because she could not bear a child. She vowed that if God would give her a son, she would dedicate him to God as a Nazarene. When the boy, whom she named Samuel, was born, Hannah gave him over to Eli. Samuel became a prophet-judge in the kingdom of David. He sought neither power nor wealth; rather, his object was the welfare of his people.

While Minnie was growing up, she was active in the local Salvation Army. She had pledged to go and preach the Gospel and serve God in any way she was asked. Before her pregnancy, she had not fulfilled this pledge. When she married James Kennedy, she prayed to God, "Oh Lord . . . You heard Hannah's prayer of old, give me a little baby girl, I will give her unreservedly into your service, that she may preach the word I should have preached. . . ."[9]

Aimee Elizabeth Kennedy was born on October 9, 1890. Three weeks after her birth, despite the Methodist leanings of Aimee's father and the icy snow flurries that were falling, Minnie Kennedy gathered up her baby girl and took her to a Salvation Army worship service. At the age of six weeks, Aimee was promoted to the Army platform and dedicated. Her mother fulfilled her promise. Aimee was publicly consecrated to God.

With both of her parents filled with religious conviction, young Aimee, whether she was aware of it or not, was already anointed as a child in God's service. A remarkable coincidence or a forecast, Aimee was born within days of the death of Catherine Booth, the sainted wife of William Booth, founder of the Salvation Army.

MINNIE AND THE SALVATION ARMY

At the time of Aimee's birth, Minnie Kennedy was hardly more than a child herself. Her father had died when she was an adolescent and her mother was sickly. One day, Minnie heard that the Salvation Army was coming to town to "take prisoners for the King," as Aimee put it in her autobiography.[10] Minnie, then twelve, was excited and begged her mother to take her to London, Ontario, to see the "Army." With impressionable eyes and ears, Minnie was fascinated by the three Salvation Army women who preached the divine call. Dressed in blue, the devout women got down on their knees and asked God to help them save souls for Jesus. After praying, their joyful voices rang with heavenly glory and they offered onlookers and would-be converts an invitation: "Oh! Say—will you go to the Eden above?" Minnie's heart melted with adoration and she answered, "I will go."[11]

Minnie was enthralled with the women in blue uniforms and their dedication and religious zeal. She pledged herself to Jesus and joined the corps. She became a sergeant major and

THE SALVATION ARMY

On a bright August day in 1917, Commander Evangeline (Eva) Booth left New York City for the front lines of World War I in France. She and the first of two hundred fifty Salvation Army volunteers entertained Allied troops with their cheerful brand of "seven-days-a-week" Christianity. After World War I, Booth was reluctant to accept thanks, saying, "The Salvation Army had no new success; we only did the old thing in an old way."*

The American people nevertheless were indebted to the organization's work. The government subscribed an unprecedented $13 million to clear "Army" war debts for canteens, hostels, rest rooms, and the care and accommodations given to returning troops.

This was not the first tribute for Booth and the Salvation Army. In the aftermath of the devastating San Francisco earthquake of 1906, she led a mass meeting in Union Square, New York, and raised over twelve thousand dollars for Salvation Army relief work.

Evangeline Booth was born on Christmas Day, 1865, the daughter of Salvation Army founder William Booth. In 1865, William Booth had begun a mission in the impoverished East End of London. Accompanied by his wife, Catherine, the former Methodist minister reached out to the most downtrodden members of society, preaching the Gospel and providing food and shelter for the homeless. He encountered countless incidents of violence but never veered from his mission. To enhance the effect and impression of the Salvation Army, he incorporated paramilitary ranks and navy blue uniforms and caps. In 1880, he sent George Scott Railton to New York to spread the Army's message to the United States. The Army made its way along the East Coast and into Canada. It was there that Aimee Semple McPherson first became involved.

Aimee's mother, Minnie Kennedy, dedicated Aimee to the Salvation Army when Aimee was six weeks old. Aimee grew up attending regular meetings. In New York City, Aimee met Commander Eva Booth and must have admired the woman's often flamboyant appearance and dramatic sermons—techniques Aimee would later use in her own career. Over the following years, like Commander Booth, Sister Aimee wore costumes based on the themes of her sermons. Booth's ladies wore navy blue uniforms. Sister Aimee's "saints" dressed in white—like angels.

Today, there are three hundred Salvation Army corps and numerous community centers and social service units throughout the world.

*Source: Salvation Army Collectibles (June 2003). Available online at *http://www.sacollectables.com.*

participated in the Salvation Army's numerous activities. She trudged miles to assist in "outpost" duties, visiting the sick, delivering food, and selling the *War Cry*—the Army's official publication. When her mother's condition worsened and death seemed imminent, she gave Minnie a choice—to live with her uncle Joseph Clark, a wealthy lumberman, or to live with the Salvation Army captain and his wife, who was Minnie's spiritual godmother. Minnie chose to go to Lindsey, Ontario, to stay at the Army headquarters.

Through a series of circumstances, Minnie became ill and moved to Ingersoll to recover. There, she learned that the wife of farmer James Kennedy was seriously ill and in need of a live-in nurse. Thirteen-year-old Minnie applied for the job and was accepted. After the woman's death, Minnie stayed on, and a year later, she married James Morgan Kennedy—he was fifty and she was fifteen. Less than five years later, God answered Minnie's prayers, and little Aimee was born.

EARLY LIFE AT HOME

Irish-American James Kennedy was both a farmer and a road engineer. While his wife took part in the godly duties of the Salvation Army, he was a devout Methodist. Their religious differences, however, did not appear to cause any family friction. Young Aimee attended the Methodist church as well as Salvation Army meetings.

James Kennedy adored Aimee and taught her to play the pump organ, ride horses, and ice skate. He shared his knowledge of nature with her and helped Aimee develop an interest in wild birds and flowers. They played children's games together, and he taught her about working the farm.

Mother Minnie shaped Aimee's earliest religious experience. She saw to it that her daughter studied the Bible and learned the Scriptures. By the time Aimee entered Dereham Public School in 1896, she knew all the Christian songs and hymns. Both parents indulged their only child with love and made sure she developed extensive biblical knowledge.

As Aimee advanced in school, she began to enjoy reading novels. Her favorites were the tales of Elsie Dinsmore, a model of obedience and piety. Aimee enjoyed acting, singing, and dancing. She sang in the Methodist choir. When she was twelve, she won a gold medal in a public-speaking contest sponsored by the Woman's Christian Temperance Union (WCTU). Aimee was invited to participate in holiday plays and other school events. As she grew older, she began to listen to and play the popular ragtime music of the day.

Sarah Bernhardt, a glamorous international actress of this period, was a huge success in both European theaters and on the American stage. Many young women were attracted to the lifestyle of the beautiful and talented French actress. Her performances in *La Tosca*, Victor Hugo's romantic *La Tisbe*, and the bold French production of *Hamlet* were famous on both continents. Her charm and style were mimicked by many girls—and Aimee was one of them. Disturbed by the changes going on in conservative rural farm life, pastors sometimes referred to moving pictures, dances, ragtime, and popular novels as "the work of the devil."

QUESTIONING HER BELIEFS

Theater personalities were not the only thing that posed a threat to young people's Christian beliefs. In 1905, Aimee entered Ingersoll Collegiate High School. Her studies included history, literature, French, algebra, and an introduction to Darwinism. What a shock it must have been for a devout Christian like Aimee to read Charles Darwin's *The Origin of Species* (1859). His revolutionary theory announced that, from the earliest and simplest forms of life, human beings evolved—which meant that humans were the highest form of life, but were also a cousin of the chimpanzee. As Darwin explained: "All individuals of the same species, and all the species of the same genus, or even higher group, must have descended from common parents; and therefore, in however distant and isolated parts of the world they are now found, they must in the course of successive generations have passed from some one part to the others." [12]

If Darwin's theory was any danger to Aimee's religious beliefs, ready to add to her confusion was Voltaire, a French writer of the seventeenth century who had been imprisoned several times for his controversial writings. Voltaire was a deist. Deism is a belief in God along with a belief in a rational "religion of nature." Deists oppose the orthodox beliefs of Christianity that assert that God influences the world he created. Voltaire believed that God was the source of the universe and natural law but did not intervene in the affairs of the world. According to his theory, the only religious duty of humanity was to be virtuous.

The last anti-Christian bombshell to challenge Aimee's religious beliefs came from the statement of a local Ingersoll pastor, who declared that God's real miracles were "drugs, surgeons"— medicine to aid the sick.[13]

Aimee was an intelligent young woman who was on the school's honor role and had passed the entrance examination for Ingersoll College. At seventeen, however, her head was spinning as she tried to define her beliefs within the diverse ideas being expounded about God and the nature of human spirituality. In response to an article on evolution published in the *Family Herald and Weekly Star*, she wrote a letter in which she argued for choosing religion over science. As biographer Edith L. Blumhofer put it: "To her mind, these seemed irreconcilable alternatives . . . and the first real test of her faith."[14]

Although she had apparently taken a stand, Aimee was still confused about Darwin's theory and how it related to God. She had several religious arguments with her mother, questioning Minnie's beliefs. At one point, Aimee asked, "How do you know there is a God?"[15] Trying to help her daughter, Minnie showed her Bible verses and took her to various churches to hear other opinions. Unable to satisfy Aimee's uncertainty, she remembered her promise to God and said, "Forgive Aimee, she is still 'God's little child.'"[16]

For proof of God's existence, Aimee needed credibility. Perhaps a miracle would explain it all for her. She prayed to God for such a miracle—one that would show her the way.

Perhaps God heard Aimee's pleas for clarification, for he seems to have intervened.

ROBERT SEMPLE AND AIMEE'S
INTRODUCTION TO PENTECOSTALISM

One day while she was out driving with her father, Aimee saw a sign in a storefront window. It read: "Pentecostal Meeting—every night at eight—Robert Semple, Irish Evangelist." (Pentecost is a Christian holiday that occurs on the seventh Sunday after Easter; it commemorates the Holy Spirit's bringing grace to the Apostles.) Aimee had heard rumors that the Pentecostals shouted, even danced, while they worshiped. Pentecostalism began in the United States around the early 1900s and emphasized individual experiences of grace, spiritual gifts, evangelism, and a belief that the return of Jesus Christ was approaching.

Aimee persuaded her father to take her to the meeting. At the mission hall, she recognized some of her neighbors—middle-class people, farmers, local merchants. While looking over the small audience, her eyes stopped to focus on a tall young man with dark hair. He held the Bible and was reading from the second book of The Acts of the Apostles.

Aimee had planned to stay only a short while at the revival service—she had a play rehearsal to attend afterward. But when Robert Semple—the young man she had spotted—began to preach and read from the Bible, she lingered.

At one point in the service, he made an altar call—that is, he asked the small congregation to come forward and be baptized by the Holy Spirit and to speak in tongues. Aimee was confused. Speak in tongues? The Methodists and Salvation Army preachers didn't speak in tongues. Semple read from the Bible and clarified the action: "'Then Peter said unto them, *Repent*, and be baptized every one of you in the name of Jesus Christ for the remission of sins, and ye shall receive the gift of the Holy Ghost.'" [17]

"Repent! Repent!" he cried again in a rich, unwavering Irish accent. "It is the word of *God*, and there *is* no other way." [18]

The congregation responded with robust and joyful cries of "Hallelujah!" and "Amen!"

For Aimee, who liked to dance and often listened to popular music and read novels, Semple's words struck a chord: "If you would rather spend your time in theaters and dance halls than in Sunday school and church, then you are not of God. You are of the devil." [19] When he appeared to look directly at her and shout, "but by nature evil before God," she believed he was speaking to her. "You stand at the crossroads tonight," he went on, "one road leads to heaven, the other leads to hell. One to life, one to death." Suddenly, in the midst of the sermon, he closed his eyes and spoke in a language she did not understand—the heavenly language of God. She had asked for a miracle and, here, her prayer was being answered. [20] In his vivid sermon, Aimee had heard the power of God at work.

Aimee recalled, "From that moment . . . never did I doubt that was God . . . he had shown me my true condition . . . a lost, miserable, hell-deserving sinner." [21] Aimee realized that, if she hoped to respond to Semple's exhortations, she would have to renounce all her sinful pleasures—dancing, drama, and moving pictures, and she would have to learn to play and sing hymns rather than ragtime. In short, she would have to give up all the things she had thought she loved.

After that first revival meeting, Aimee devoured the words in her Bible and prayed on her knees. She did what the Pentecostals called "searching for God." She desperately wanted to be a Christian—a child of God—holy and consecrated. In her Bible, she found the answer: "Ask and it shall be given you; seek, and ye shall find; knock, and it shall be opened unto you. For every one that asketh receiveth; and he that seeketh findeth; and to him that knocketh it shall be opened"(Luke 11:9–13). It was as if a great voice had spoken to her and ordained her future. Yet, how could a farmer's daughter ever hope to be a soul saver for Jesus? At this time, it was only men who served as preachers.

Aimee continued to search the Bible for verification. In Acts 2:39, she found, "For the promise is unto you, and to your children, and to all that are afar off, even as many as the Lord our God shall call." She then read Acts 11:17: ". . . who was I that I could withstand God?" and Acts 19:6: "And when Paul had laid his hands upon them, the Holy Ghost came on them, and they spake with tongues, and prophesied."

Then the local Methodist minister admonished her. "These people you are associating with are in all likelihood rank fanatics," said the preacher. "What warrant have you that seeking this so-called power you may not become possessed with an evil spirit?" [22]

3

Anointed of the Holy Spirit

Then suddenly, out of my innermost
being flowed rivers of praise in other
tongues as the Spirit gave utterance . . .
—Acts of the Apostles 2:4

Aimee was intent on becoming a true Christian, but she believed that if she didn't speak in tongues, she was in grave danger of being cast into hell without mercy. At the Pentecostal mission house, she spent hours on her knees praying—"tarrying," as the Pentecostals called the process of praying and waiting for baptism. Speaking in tongues is one piece of evidence believed to demonstrate that someone has received the baptism of the Holy Spirit, and it was for this that Aimee prayed. Biographer Daniel Mark Epstein described her quest: "She felt as if she were battering her way 'through a thick stone wall that was growing as thin as tissue paper.'"[23]

Tarrying with the Pentecostals at their hall caused Aimee to miss high school classes and fall behind in her homework. As a result, her grades fell off. The school principal sent her mother a letter warning her that unless Aimee paid more attention to her studies, she would fail. It was not only the principal who voiced concern for Aimee; officers from the Salvation Army also came to the Kennedy farmhouse. They expressed surprise that Minnie Kennedy, a longtime Army worker, would allow her daughter to attend the Pentecostal mission. They pointed out that, since Minnie had worked many years for the Army, it set a bad example for other people for her to allow Aimee to associate with Pentecostals. The Army delegation believed that "her daughter should show better sense."[24]

BAPTISM IN THE HOLY SPIRIT

Minnie scolded Aimee and insisted that she return to school and not visit the Pentecostal mission again. Aimee wanted to obey her mother, but one day, snow flurries were as heavy as her heart and she changed her mind. Her desire to be baptized in the Holy Spirit was too intense. Instead of going to school, and despite her mother's forbidding, Aimee went back to the mission house. The Pentecostals welcomed her, and she decided to spend the entire day on her knees praying that God would either baptize her then and there or arrange it so that she could remain until she did receive baptism. As if in answer to her prayers, the snow flurries turned into a full-blown blizzard—telephone lines went down, trains stopped running. From Monday to Saturday, snow inundated the village and, all the while, Aimee remained on her knees. She promised God she would stay on her knees until he poured out the Holy Spirit on her—that is, until she spoke in tongues. Early Saturday morning, according to Aimee's account, she cried, "Oh, Lord God be merciful to me, a sinner! . . . the most wonderful change took place in my soul."[25]

Suddenly, without any effort on her part, she began to repeat, "Glory to Jesus! Glory to Jesus! All at once her hands began to tremble until her whole body was quivering with the power of the Holy Spirit."[26] She recalled slipping to the floor caught up and floating—speaking in tongues. Aimee was seventeen and she had been born again.

During the snowstorm, Minnie assumed that Aimee was stuck at school or at a friend's house. When Aimee returned home and

THE BIRTH OF PENTECOSTALISM

The Pentecostal, or revivalist, movement, originated in 1906 when members of the congregation of the Azusa Street Mission in Los Angeles experienced "baptism in the Holy Spirit." Pentecostals believed in the literal word of the Bible and in faith healing. Originally, the religion's appeal was to the poor and others who did not accept the formal modern theology of established Christian denominations. Pentecostalism grew rapidly in the South and in underprivileged urban areas.

Pentecostalism combines a highly emotional and informal approach to worship with an emphasis on sobriety and hard work. Its dogma stresses that the Holy Spirit is God's instrument of blessing. The religion is also concerned with the subjective side of Christian faith—personal conversion and the baptism of the Holy Spirit, accompanied by speaking in tongues. Alcohol, tobacco, dancing, the theater, and gambling are forbidden. Participation in the new church became a way for poor and blue-collar groups to improve their economic and social status and to renew their religious faith.

Pentecostalism remains one of the fastest-growing religious movements in history. Today, it has a powerful appeal in many other countries.

told her mother that she had been with the Pentecostals and had found the way to God, Minnie was very angry. Despite her mother's disapproval, Aimee was overjoyed, feeling that her burden had been lifted. She merely sang out with delight. The glory of God filled her heart. She went to the iron stove in the dining room, opened its door, and tossed in her dance shoes, ragtime music, and novels.

Minnie Kennedy was frantic and felt disgraced. For his part, Aimee's father was bewildered. They were Christians, but they did not understand speaking in tongues or the extremely conservative Pentecostal religious viewpoint. Nevertheless, they loved their daughter and were anxious to help her. Minnie took out her Bible to search for the truth. She determined that if she could find a reference to speaking in tongues, she would forgive her daughter and accept her chosen faith. All night she read until she found a phrase in Isaiah 28:11: "Nay, but by men of strange lips and with an alien tongue the Lord will speak to this people." Mother and daughter were overjoyed. Together, they danced around the kitchen table and sang, "Give me that old-time religion, It's good enough for me . . . "

Now that she was anointed with the Holy Spirit, Aimee's driving religious conviction was not slowed. She kept hearing God's voice calling her to come into the field and be a soul winner for Jesus. She also heard the objections of others— she was too young, women were not meant to be preachers, Pentecostal preachers received no salary, she would not be able to survive, and so on. Despite these negative opinions, as Aimee later recalled, she said, "I can hear my Savior calling, take your cross and follow, follow Me." [27]

MARRIAGE AND MISSIONARY WORK

During her struggles with doubters, the young Pentecostal preacher Robert Semple reappeared in her life. This time, he was not only an evangelist preacher who helped her find salvation, but he also wanted to marry her. Aimee fell in love with him. He asked Minnie Kennedy for her daughter's hand in marriage and asked God to solemnize their engagement. Nine years older than Aimee, Robert Semple also wanted his new bride to be his helpmate in preaching the Gospel and in his efforts "to rescue poor perishing souls from eternal destruction."[28] On August 12, 1908, Robert and Aimee were married. Near the end of the year, the newlyweds moved to Chicago. Robert was ordained as a minister in 1909 at the Full Gospel Assembly Church, and Aimee was ordained later that same year.

Like other Christian churches, the Pentecostals also sent out missionaries to other parts of the world. However, in 1910, they did not have the financial means to fund an official missionary program. As Ellen Hebden of the Hebden Mission in Toronto explained, "Everyone sent forth is called of God and baptized with the Holy Ghost speaking in tongues, as at Pentecost. All go forth dependent on God alone; no board or organization or suggestions of such to lessen faith in God."[29] The lack of secure funding apparently did not bother Robert and Aimee Semple. They appeared to be able to raise enough money through their preaching to survive.

Robert Semple had begun his religious training with the Hebdens while living in Canada. Toronto's large Chinese population evidently became his focus. After only a year of living in Chicago, in June 1910, the Semples set out to evangelize in China.

Without sufficient backing and as a result of of the tremendous health obstacles they would face—cholera, dysentery, and malaria—three months later, their glorious adventure and burning desire to answer God's call ended with Robert's tragic death from dysentery. Aimee returned to the United States penniless—a grieving window with a one-month-old sick baby. Upon her arrival in San Francisco, however, she was presented with an envelope containing sixty-five dollars, which had been donated by the ship's other passengers. She and baby Roberta boarded a train for New York City. There, she joined her mother, who had left James Kennedy and the farm and moved to the city to devote her life to the Salvation Army.

WORKING WITH THE ARMY

Minnie Kennedy persuaded the Army to take in Aimee, who went to work standing on street corners, clapping a tambourine and trying to save sinners. She was allowed to keep half the money she collected. She also worked in the Army kitchen serving meals to the poor.

On Sundays, Aimee Semple attended the Glad Tidings Mission, a Pentecostal church in the heart of New York City. Its pastors were Robert and Marie Brown. Aimee observed and no doubt admired and gained confidence from watching Marie Brown preach the Gospel right alongside her husband. During one of the services, Aimee told the congregation about her tragic experience in China. Although the church members took up a collection for her, she felt shame and discomfort. She worried that "they questioned the authenticity of her call to Hong Kong, that somehow Robert's death had been a punishment for her misguided inspiration."[30]

Grieving for her husband and alone, Aimee Semple decided to return to Chicago and work in the church where he had preached. The Chicago smoke and congestion, however, combined with her poor living quarters, made life stressful and did not help either Aimee or Roberta. When Roberta stopped eating, Aimee wired her father for money and returned to the farm. Her mother left New York City and also returned to the farm to care for her daughter and the baby.

The atmosphere of the farm and the support of her parents helped Aimee recover and baby Roberta's health to improve. Aimee Semple then returned to Chicago. But her future was still uncertain. She took Roberta to a doctor, and he told Aimee that the child's health would never get stronger without "a good home and plenty of fresh air, warmth, and care."[31] His advice convinced her to return to New York City. Her mother returned to the city, too.

SECOND MARRIAGE AND A NEWBORN SON

Faced with an uncertain future, desperation, and loneliness, Aimee Semple met Harold McPherson. On February 28, 1912, she married the young accountant. Mack, as he was called, was from Providence, Rhode Island. His mother owned a boarding-house there. After they were married, the couple moved to Providence with his parents. Social convention of the day dictated that Aimee give priority to her position as a wife and mother rather than to any career ambitions she might have. In July, she became pregnant, and the following spring, on March 23, 1913, a boy named Rolf McPherson was born.

Aimee tried to settle down to normal home life, but the call to Christian service remained constant—the voice persisted. Occasionally, Aimee evangelized but, to her, this was not sufficient to answer God's call. Yet, while she tried to be a wife, mother, and a sometime preacher, her health declined. Following Rolf's birth and still overwhelmed with grief and confusion, she grew weaker and weaker. Today, her illness might be identified as postpartum depression. Heart trouble and hemorrhaging from her stomach added to her woes. Her appendix was removed. She had a hysterectomy, and on what she expected to be her deathbed, after her second operation within two years, she answered "yes" to God's call. Almost immediately thereafter, she was healed.[32] Aimee later saw this concession to God as the reason she recovered from her near-death experience.[33]

Consumed with the need to follow God's instructions and the belief that God was leading her, she wired her mother for money. Late one night, alone in her house, she packed up her two children and took the midnight train to Canada. For the second time in her life, she was setting forth to obey God and preach his word. Unlike when she had accompanied Robert Semple to China, though, this time, she was going it alone.

Upon her return to Canada, Aimee attended a Pentecostal camp meeting and asked God to forgive her for straying. Her dedication to God and her willingness to join in the camp revivals caught the attention of Mrs. J. E. Sharp. When the meet-ings ended, Mrs. Sharp asked Aimee to conduct a revival in a small hall in Mount Forest, Ontario. Aimee's dramatic preaching and dedicated Pentecostal spirit overflowed. People crowded the hall to hear her. To hold a larger congregation, a tent was erected. Night after night, it was filled. Healings were made and many lost souls saved. Those who could not get inside stood outside and listened to her from there.

In the midst of one of the meetings, Harold McPherson appeared with his suitcase. His wife was "radiantly happy."[34] He received the baptism of the Holy Spirit, spoke in tongues, and admitted that this was indeed his wife's true calling. At the conclusion of the Mount Forest revival, the couple returned to the United States. Aimee began to raise money to purchase her own tent so she could hold revival meetings of her own.

4

Corona! Corona!
A Healing Ministry

*Her faith had moved her into a channel of life
where faith could move mountains, and did.*

—Biographer Daniel Mark Epstein

President Woodrow Wilson was reelected the twenty-eighth president of United States in 1916. He won by a slim margin under the slogan: HE KEPT US OUT OF WAR. This was a reference to World War I, the devastating conflict that had been raging in Europe since 1914. The threat of the United States' entering the war had increased after the British ocean liner *Lusitania* was sunk in 1915 by a German submarine. President Wilson's attempt to mediate the war ended the following spring and, on April 6, 1917, he secured a declaration of war against Germany.

In the United States, there were less fearsome, but nevertheless eventful, happenings. That autumn of 1917, a young woman with dark eyes and auburn hair embarked on a lifelong odyssey that few women had ever undertaken. Until Aimee Kennedy stood at the altar, there had been few women evangelists. Objections came from fundamentalist preachers who asserted that women's emotional dispositions made them unfit for preaching. According to these people, a woman's place was in the home—cleaning the house and caring for the family. A recent exception to this line of thinking was the well-known Christian advocate Evangeline Booth, commander of the Salvation Army. As a child, Aimee had heard Commander Eva speak and, most likely, she was inspired by the woman's soul-winning sermons and dramatic presentations. Much later, Aimee Semple McPherson would regard "female preachers as a 'sign of the times'" and insist that a woman "must preach to fulfill the Scriptures . . . if she really feels it to be her task."[35]

Christian tent revivals were becoming more common and growing in popularity. Small tents for housing the visiting congregation were illuminated with kerosene lanterns. People teamed up to cook and share meals. The weeklong religious gatherings were held in a larger adjoining tent.

During one of these meetings, people were baptized and accepted Jesus Christ as their savior. After the baptism, some of the converts spoke in tongues. Biblical readings kindled Aimee's desire to evangelize and help others achieve salvation.

She joined other converts and prayed to God to be forgiven for straying from his grace. According to her autobiography, at one meeting, she felt God's forgiveness, rose from her knees, and began to speak in tongues. She then interpreted her message for the congregation and laid her hands on the heads of others so that they, too, might receive the Holy Spirit. After the service ended, empowered with God's will, she asked the preacher, "Is there anything I can do for Jesus?"

He answered, "Why, I'm sure I don't know."

As she left the tent, she asked two other people if there was anything she could do to for Jesus. Each replied that there was nothing they knew of. Finally, she asked another man, and he replied, "Why sure—can you wash dishes?"

"Why, certainly I can. Every woman can do that."[36]

He pointed to two washtubs filled with dirty plates and silverware.

Impervious to this insult, Aimee continued to ask other people what she could do for Jesus. Already she had played the piano, directed the choir, and cleaned up the kitchen. On the last day of the meeting, only one pastor remained. When she again asked what she could do for Jesus, he answered, "Can you preach?" Suddenly, Aimee had been given the opportunity to preach her first sermon. Exultation must have swept through her, for she recalled, "I was weak and dizzy from the sheer joy and glory of it."[37]

PREACHING THE GOSPEL

For the next two years, Aimee worked by day and prayed by night. She wandered up and down the East Coast, spreading the Gospel. Beneath tattered tents or on street corners, she conducted her ministry. Sometimes her audience was only a handful of men, women, and boys. She prayed for more souls to save. A humble few were not sufficient. She believed Jesus wanted her to do more—that he was always urging her, "Preach the word! Preach the word!"[38] But how would she be able to reach so many more people? She fell to her knees and asked God to give her instruction.

She was on her knees when she heard the words, "Corona, Corona." At first, she thought this was a reference to a popular typewriter brand of the day. She explained, "I had been asking the Lord for a typewriter and thought he was going to give me a Corona as the word keep ringing in my ears."[39] She needed a

UNDER THE BIG TOP

The billowing expanse of canvas—the Big Top—beckoned people to midsummer gatherings. Souls to be saved, healings to be made, God's message—this was the essence of a tent revival. Aimee, like dozens of other evangelists across the United States, held many outdoor revivals. Compared with the price of renting a hall, tenting was relatively inexpensive. It also gave the audience a feeling of excitement and warm enthusiasm. The sounds of preaching and the joyous music could be heard for blocks.

Months before the opening of her Oakland campaign, a local committee began to make plans. By the final meeting, 500 to 600 volunteers were ready to serve. Several thousand dollars were pledged—about half of the total campaign expenses. Flyers and newspaper advertising preceded Aimee's arrival.

On the morning of the event, she arrived by train. A large crowd greeted her with bouquets of flowers and hearty cheers. Cameras flashed as newspaper reporters and photographers captured the action. After a short welcome and hymns from the chorus, she and the committee chair stepped into the front car. Large platform trucks draped in green-and-white banners announced the tent meeting. Riding in the trucks were the band members with their shining instruments and the singers from the chorus. As the parade traveled toward the meeting ground, a long stream of cars joined it.

The tent was set up and sawdust scattered over the bare ground. Inside, a wood platform was installed for the visiting clergy and the choir. Unless electricity was available, lighting was supplied by calcium carbide lanterns.

Decorating the stage were baskets of flowers and flags. There was a large portrait of Jesus at the crucifixion. A borrowed grand piano sat in the band area.

typewriter to prepare her sermons and write letters. This time, though, Aimee was about to discover that God's plans for her future were far greater than giving her a typewriter. Struggling to broaden her ministry, she had sent letters to various churches along the Atlantic seaboard, asking if she might come and hold a revival. One reply that came back caught her eye. Its postmark was from Corona, Long Island, New York. Was this a sign from

The first meeting began on Saturday night. The tent tabernacle was filled to capacity, the wooden benches were crowded, and many people were standing both inside and out. Special police ringed the exterior to prevent any trouble but not one was needed—despite the thousands of people crowded together, the revival was completely peaceful. The chorus and the band began and soon the audience caught the refrain. A chorus of amens and hallelujahs echoed outside. After preaching and more singing, Aimee made the altar call. Sawdust and dirt flew as scores of people went forward to seek salvation, taking seats on the seven long altar benches. Others knelt at the feet of the crucified Jesus. Many were weeping, hands raised, seeking and finding Jesus as their savior.

Throughout the entire two weeks, there were three meetings a day. There were special meetings for the old and the young. The oldest dozen people over the ages of eighty and ninety were called to the platform. Hymns that had been popular fifty to sixty years ago were then sung. At the services for children, there was a chorus of singing young people dressed in white. The orchestra was composed of children, and the solos and quartets were performed by young people. Aimee's sermon was directed to the youth and she followed with an altar call. Afterward, children received Bibles and gifts of clothing, food, or toys, depending on their economic need.

During the campaign, newspapers carried daily stories and photos, and the radio broadcast her sermons. Donations came from the audience and from outlying areas. In Oakland, there was a large public swimming pool where a water baptismal service was held. Baptizing five candidates at a time, the service lasted for two hours. Hundreds were baptized in all.

God? It certainly wasn't from the Smith-Corona typewriter company, offering her a typewriter. Instead, it was a letter asking her to hold a revival.

> Dear Sister McPherson:
>
> For two years I have been lying on my face before God beseeching him to send a revival to Corona.
>
> He has now revealed to me that a mighty city-sweeping revival is to be sent through your ministry. . . .
>
> Your room is all prepared. Come immediately. Expecting great things of the Lord.[40]

In response to the invitation, Aimee left her daughter, Roberta, with her mother, and her son, Rolf, with her grandmother Kennedy, then set out to begin her work.

The village of Corona was a working neighborhood in north-central Queens, New York, located off the Long Island Rail Road line. The major local industry was the manufacturing of china and Tiffany glass.

There was a surprise in store for Aimee Semple McPherson when she arrived at the home of the woman who had sent her the letter. The gracious lady who answered the door—the one who had sent the letter—was black. Until now, Aimee had seen only a few black people in her life, but she knew no color bounds. The smiling woman welcomed her and said, "Is y'all Sistah McPherson been preachin in a big tent?"[41] *Sister* is a term often used in Pentecostal churches to denote a female member's ties to the congregation, and it increasingly became a moniker used by the public to denote Aimee's religious status.

Aimee nodded and the woman sat her down at the kitchen table and served tea. Aimee soon learned that the woman who had invited her to preach had made no preparations at all for holding a revival. She would only say, "Ah's got it all prayed through now."[42]

For several days, she and Sister Aimee walked the streets of Corona, searching for an auditorium or hall in which to hold the revival. Local Christian ministers had warned their congregations against Aimee's "hypnotism." Some people were frightened; they worried that she would put them into a religious trance. Many pastors of other denominations feared and shunned the robust Pentecostal revivals that lasted all day and into the night. The Pentecostals were called "Holy Rollers" and were known for their outrageous preaching, boisterous singing, loud amens and hallelujahs, and for their converts who often spoke in tongues. Discouraged but not thwarted, Sister Aimee continued to search for a location and prayed that God would help her find a place. One man offered her the use of his saloon, which she respectfully turned down.

The pastor of the Swedish Methodist Episcopal Church finally answered her prayers. He asked her to come and conduct some meetings. On the first night, there were few people in attendance. Soon, however, word spread around town about the pretty woman preacher. Curious people from all different backgrounds flocked to the church. Some stood on boxes and looked in the church windows; others, too timid to come in, peeked in through the doorway. From outlying villages, people came on horseback or in horse-drawn buggies. The congregation overflowed the church's available space.

After watching her preach, another minister, W. K. Bouton, wanted a share of the revival crowds, too, and invited Aimee to his Corona Free Gospel Church. He must have been skeptical, because he asked the congregation, "How many believe they had not received the baptism of the Holy Spirit and would like to receive it?" Would-be converts came down the aisles. One woman, widely respected within the Christian community, fainted and was given water. Upon regaining consciousness, she began to speak in tongues. The church walls rocked with rejoicing, and the next night, there was even greater attendance. Pastor Bouton told his wife, "Sister Aimee is honest, and she sure knows her Bible."[43]

During her first sermons in Corona, the church pastors had told Sister Aimee what they wanted her to preach. An assembly of ministers and deacons even sat behind her on the pulpit to observe her work. She recalled that "the dignified clergymen 'sat like human interrogation marks at the very thought of a woman preaching the Gospel.'"[44] Undaunted by their presence, she proceeded to state that the Christian church had lost the gifts of the Holy Spirit—the powers of prophecy, speaking in tongues, and divine healing; it was her inspired belief that God would restore these gifts before the second coming of Jesus. Indeed, she claimed, he was restoring them even now in Corona, Long Island.

Pleased with the large number of converts being baptized with the Holy Spirit, the clergy graciously allowed Sister Aimee to preach as she wished. Pastor Bouton himself got down on his knees. So frantically did he pray that he, too, spoke in tongues and collapsed on the floor. After waking, he claimed to have seen God.

Aimee laced her preaching with words from Hebrews 13:8: "Jesus Christ the same yesterday, and today and forever, that he still lives to save and heal and baptize with His Holy Spirit." This biblical phrase became the touchstone of many of her services. Music and joyful singing, including songs such as "Bringing in the Sheaves" and "Give Me Some Old Time Religion," were also a big part of her revivals.

There was one thing still missing, though. Aimee had never personally prayed for the sick to heal them. On one memorable November evening, that changed. During the altar call at the Free Gospel Church, a teenager on crutches suddenly came forward. She was bowed and twisted with advanced rheumatoid arthritis, a painful, incurable inflammation of the body's joints. Aimee was doubtful at first that she could help the girl. Nevertheless, she prayed for the power of Jesus Christ to heal the physically impaired and repeated the words of James 5:14–15: "Is any among you sick? Let him call for the elders of the church; and let them pray over him, anointing him with oil in the name of the Lord; And the prayer of faith shall save the sick, and the Lord shall rise him up; and if he have committed sins, they shall be forgiven him."

The teenager's name was Louise Messnick. By faith a Catholic, Louise had decided to come to the service after she heard about Sister Aimee's remarkable preaching. Tearful, the girl slowly made her way down the aisle, taking one painful step after another, until she reached the altar. Sister Aimee raised her arms, her face flushed, and prayed for God to heal the young woman.

According to Aimee Semple McPherson's own account, she had planned to come down to the front seat where she could pray for the girl without being conspicuous. But Louise, unable to kneel, was placed in the central minister's seat with the aid of friends. "I tried to tell myself that the kinder thing to do was to make it as inconspicuous as possible," Sister Aimee later wrote about her misgivings.[45]

Louise was anointed with the Holy Spirit and baptized. Sister Aimee told her to lift up her hands and praise the Lord. Slowly, Louise raised her arms until both hands were free. Her chin and neck began to move and turn and she looked heavenward. In minutes, she was standing on her feet, holding on to the chancel rail. As her limbs straightened, she began to walk. She threw her crutches down, praised God, and walked on her own out of the church. After that day, Louise never left the Pentecostal religion. Years later, Sister Aimee said she saw Louise again—a healthy, giggly, and devout woman.

At the conclusion of Sister Aimee's last Corona service, Pastor Bouton announced to the congregation that a table had been set up near the altar with an open Bible on it. The grateful were invited to come forward and make a donation to Sister Aimee. When it was all over, the Bible was buried beneath a mound of dollars and coins—enough to take Aimee, her children, and her mother to Aimee's next meeting in Florida. This was the beginning of Aimee Semple McPherson's long and successful healing ministry.

5

Shout! For the Lord Has Given Aimee the City!

They say, "The world is my oyster."
Well, I wouldn't put it that way.
But the world is my little problem.

—From Aimee Semple McPherson's
"This is my Task" sermon, 1939

When Aimee Semple McPherson began preaching in earnest, a woman in the pulpit was not only a novelty, but a target for criticism by other ministers. Many orthodox ministers were even critical of male evangelists. Dwight Laymen Moody, Charles Haddon Spurgeon, and Billy Sunday were evangelists who challenged traditional religious methods with showy, theatrical performances—a contradiction to conventional views. Moody and Spurgeon's dynamics were well known in the nineteenth century and, although they were censured for their vibrant sermons, Moody founded the world-famous Moody Institute and Spurgeon, who drew an estimated ten thousand people to his London services, wrote voluminous printed works. His sermons remain popular even today.

Because of her own lively revivals, the press would later characterize Aimee Semple McPherson as another Billy Sunday. Unlike her contemporaries, though, her messages showed the face of a loving God. With outstretched arms and joyful words, she told listeners about heaven, a place people wanted to be, and she talked about serving Jesus as the only way of life that offered true fulfillment.

Not only were early evangelists criticized for their religious fervor, but they were sometimes physically attacked by other Christians who disapproved of their methods. Sister Aimee was undaunted by such nonbelievers. She continued to believe that traditional methods of teaching the Gospel were lifeless and unproductive.

SISTER AIMEE'S REVIVALS

Knowing that she had to keep her promise to the Lord, Aimee took her ministry one step further and moved away from the solemn, gloomy, and archaic sermons of ordinary preachers. People wanted to hear about Jesus Christ, but more importantly, they wanted to know about the living and empowering Christ of the present day. He was, as Aimee often said, "Jesus Christ, Yesterday, and Today, and Forever." Her sermons were backed up by choirs of heavenly singing; music played by tambourines, drums, triangles, and guitars; and the simple words of the Gospel. Choruses of amens and hallelujahs punctuated her speeches. Eyewitness Nancy Bastajian remembered, "Aimee's revivals were not only for healing and soul saving, but they were entertaining as well."[46]

When Sister Aimee first began to travel around the eastern part of the country evangelizing, she did not ask for regular church offerings. She was informed by a farmer after one revival that she wasn't a traditional preacher. When she asked why, the reply was, "You've been here a whole week and have never taken a single collection."[47] The farmer then went into the audience. Holding out his straw hat, he joked and cajoled members of the congregation to give. The offerings were generous enough that, in 1918, Aimee Semple McPherson was able to purchase the so-called Gospel Car—a Packard. On one side of the car was painted the phrase, JESUS IS COMING SOON—GET READY! The other side said, WHERE WILL YOU SPEND ETERNITY?

With the Gospel Car and continuing donations from the collection plate, Sister Aimee was able to extend her travels and publicly announce her revivals. When she arrived in a new town, before each meeting, she advertised the time and place, passed out handbills, and urged everyone to come and be anointed with the Holy Spirit. People came in ever-increasing numbers to hear this remarkable woman evangelist. Attendants often overflowed the local church tabernacles and halls. Often, Sister Aimee had to share a hall with another event. On one occasion, she actually spoke from a boxing ring—although there were no matches going on, of course.

A TENT AND A GROWING MINISTRY

Aimee Semple McPherson was determined to reach more people with God's message, and the next step was to buy a tent where she could fit much larger audiences. With fifteen hundred dollars in hand, she approached a seller who asked for two thousand dollars. Sister Aimee bargained with the man, telling him that the tent was going to be used for God's work. Obviously intimidated, he settled for the fifteen hundred. When the tent was delivered and installed for the service that was about to begin, there were dozens of rips and tears in the canvas. Despite the tent's tattered condition, she used it to hold her first meeting. The following day, willing supporters came with thread and large needles and patched up all the holes.

With her newly repaired tent, Sister Aimee extended her travels, and with her mother and two small children, she moved from town to town. She always seemed to take in enough money from the collection plate to keep going.

During the winters of 1917 and 1918, with a growing entourage of volunteers, Sister Aimee pitched the tent in several large Florida cities, including St. Petersburg. Her husband, Harold, was still traveling with her, despite their growing separation.

Meetings usually went off without any mishap. At one revival, however, there was no electricity to light the tent. Always prepared, Sister Aimee carried a calcium carbide lighting system. Evidently, there was a defect in her equipment, and while she was making adjustments, it blew up. Her face was blackened, her eyelashes and eyebrows were gone, and her hair was singed. Meanwhile, flames threatened to destroy the tent. It was still early and there were few people in the tent, and fortunately, she was able to stop the fire. Her surrounding followers applied baking soda to her face, and she tried to relieve the pain by dunking her face in cold water.

When people began to fill the tent, Sister Aimee wondered how she would be able to walk the aisles. She always liked to begin a service this way so she could catch the spirit of the audience and decide what tone her sermon should take. She entered the tent, her dress splattered with water, and stepped to the platform, raising one hand. From her burned lips she exclaimed, "I praise the Lord that he heals me and takes the pain away!"[48] The audience shouted "Hallelujah!" According to Aimee, instantly, before the eyes of the congregation, her red burns faded and the white blisters that had formed on her face disappeared. By the end of the service, her face had resumed its usual appearance.

THE BRIDAL CALL

With the tent, the handbills, and her growing popularity, Sister Aimee's next ambitious project was the publication of *The Bridal Call*, a four-page country newsletter that stressed the second coming of Christ. Its title was taken from the New Testament parable in Matthew 25:1–13, about ten virgins going to meet a bridegroom. As they left, all ten women took lamps with them, but only five of them were wise enough to fill their lamps with oil. As the bridegroom arrived, the virgins went to light their lamps. Those without oil had to run out to buy some. While they were gone, the five virgins who already had oil went with the bridegroom, and the door was locked behind them. Later, when the other five maidens returned, they shouted for the bridegroom to open the door. He responded that he did not know them. The meaning, of course, was that a person must always be prepared, for no one can know when he or she will die.

The first issue of *The Bridal Call* was published in June 1917 in Savannah, Georgia. After three months, Sister Aimee made arrangements to combine with the Christian Worker's Union to put out an expanded periodical. It was filled with her sermons, news, photographs of her campaigns, poems, and other articles of interest. When she passed a mailbox, the Gospel Car would stop and she'd leave a copy of *The Bridal Call*. It had a subscription price of twenty-five cents per year. Sister Louise, a volunteer, often took Aimee's dictation and helped with the publication.

A TRANSCONTINENTAL JOURNEY

While Aimee Semple McPherson was gaining national prominence, the United States had entered World War I (known then as the Great War). Her touring tent revivals might have continued, but she fell ill and underwent two surgeries. When a severe influenza epidemic swept across the United States and Europe, actually killing more people than the war itself, she held back from her travels. Her eight-year-old daughter was struck with the influenza virus and came close to death. The "saints" (Aimee's followers) gathered to pray for her. Roberta, who at one point appeared to be improving, went to see her mother, who was preaching at the Harlem Casino in New York City. There, she asked to give her testimony, and thanked God for saving her and for revealing his glory to her. Unfortunately, Roberta had not fully recovered. When her mother learned of her serious condition, she got down on her knees and prayed to God to save her daughter's life. According to Aimee, he answered: "I will give you a little home—a nest for your babies—out in Los Angeles, California, where they can play and be happy and go to school and have the home surroundings of other children."[49] Sister Aimee had not completely recovered from her own surgeries, but she was determined to follow God's instructions and head west. Her husband would not go with her. (They would divorce in 1921.) With God-given orders, she began preparations for a transcontinental trip by car.

Hearing of her plans, a pastor in Tulsa, Oklahoma, requested that Sister Aimee stop and hold a revival. Just as she, her mother, and the children were ready to leave, however, he sent a telegram informing her that all the churches in the area were shut down because of the influenza epidemic. Sister Aimee asked God for guidance. She later said God assured her to leave at once and that the day she arrived, the ban would be lifted and the churches would reopen.

On October 23, 1918, the long trip to California began. Aimee had traded in the Packard Gospel Car and bought a brand-new, seven-seater Oldsmobile touring car. Her trademark words, Jesus is Coming Soon—Get Ready, and Where Will You Spend Eternity?, were painted in six-inch gold lettering on either side. Cooking utensils, blankets, and suitcases were piled inside. Several custom-made brackets were strapped onto the trunk lid. Additional brackets were welded to the fenders to support folding cots and a tent for the children. Minnie Kennedy and the children sat in the backseat. Aimee drove, while Sister Louise navigated. Traveling at twenty-five miles an hour, they started at sunrise and drove late into the evening. At night, the front seat was folded back and a canvas blanket draped over the car. They camped by the side of the road, unless they were invited to stay in private residences.

Along the way, Sister Aimee would stop and hand out literature and *The Bridal Call*. Local newspapers began to take notice of her. Sister Aimee and her traveling companions

THE INFLUENZA EPIDEMIC OF 1918

World War I was winding down in 1918 and peace was imminent. Thousands of American and foreign soldiers had been killed or injured fighting the Germans and their allies. Casualties were high and conditions were insufferable. To make matters even worse, another dreadful catastrophe occurred. Half of all U.S. soldiers who died in Europe fell victim to the influenza virus. Despite the devastating war, the greatest loss of life during this period ultimately resulted from infectious disease in the form of the flu.*

Influenza first appeared in Boston in September 1918. As men across the country joined the military, they brought the virus with them, and it often spread to those with whom they came into contact. Almost 200,000 people died in the month of October alone. When the war ended in November 1918, there was a resurgence of the disease as large gatherings of people came together to celebrate. That winter, the flu was epidemic—millions were infected and thousands died.

Public health ordinances were issued and gauze masks were distributed to be worn in public. Churches closed for public safety, railroads did not accept passengers without signed medical certificates, and some places required people to present a signed certificate to enter. Medical facilities, doctors, and health-care workers were pressed into service—yet physicians were helpless against the sickness, since it was a virus that could not be fought with medication. The alarmingly high death rate actually caused a shortage of coffins, morticians, and gravediggers.

were photographed beside the Oldsmobile, and stories talked about the evangelist and her transcontinental trip to Los Angeles. People flocked to see her. At one point, an army convoy filled with soldiers passed by and Sister Aimee blessed them all.

There were few who did not understand the messages written on the sides of the Oldsmobile. People wanted to hear more. Some had questions they wanted answered, while others wanted to be blessed and receive salvation. People believed Sister Aimee had the answers.

The disease was recorded as the most devastating epidemic in world history. More people died of influenza in a single year than had died in four years of the so-called Black Death—an epidemic of bubonic plague between 1347 and 1351. Children skipped rope to the rhyme:

I had a little bird,

Its name was Enza

I opened the window,

And in-flu-enza.

Influenza circled the globe through North America, Europe, Asia, Africa, Brazil, and the South Pacific. The origins of the disease were unknown. Some people thought it was a biological weapon being used by the Germans, the result of trench warfare, or an effect of the use of mustard gases in battle. Its true origin is not precisely known even today. It is thought to have originated in China in a rare genetic shift of the influenza virus. Recently, the virus has been reconstructed from the tissue of a dead soldier and is being genetically characterized.**

 * Source: The American Medical Association final edition of 1918, "The Influenza Pandemic of 1918." Available online at *http://www.stanford.edu/group/virus/uda/*.

** Source: Stanford Education Group/Virus.

The farther she traveled across the nation, the more the news of her ministry preceded her. Homes were opened to her and meals were offered. The travelers' clothes and muddy car were washed.

When they reached Tulsa, the churches had opened, just as Sister Aimee claimed God had said. She held meetings and visited and prayed for the many people who were sick with influenza. She blessed everyone who sought the Lord. She preached on street corners and in iron works, and she sang as she tried to save souls from sin and shame.

When word reached a town that Sister Aimee was coming, the Pentecostal "saints"—Aimee's followers—waited excitedly. In Oklahoma City, there were many requests for revivals and meetings among the Indians. With winter approaching, though, and the weather forecast calling for heavy snow, Aimee Semple McPherson hastened on. Through rain and snow, on and on she drove, passing farmland, crossing swollen rivers, climbing mountains, and getting a first glimpse of cactus and sage. All the while, she continued to hand out literature, witness for Jesus, and leave copies of *The Bridal Call*. When she and her companions reached California and drove on to Los Angeles, the car's odometer registered over four thousand miles.

A NEW HOME IN LOS ANGELES

Unlike other cities where she had held revivals, Los Angeles was rife with evangelists. "Satan's own false prophets are converging . . . by the dozens," said Pastor Jacobs, who preached to a small congregation in Victoria Hall. "Cultists in this town preach salvation through everything from weight lifting to orgies of the flesh—it's unthinkable, abysmal. One impostor teaches mind reading as the road to God." Then he added, "Which is, by the way, precisely why we've invited you here, Mrs. McPherson. . . . God has used you to bring salvation and Holy Spirit baptism, and that's proof enough your work is of God." [50]

Two days later, Aimee Semple McPherson opened her revival in Victoria Hall. The upstairs meeting room seated seven hundred. Within days, there were such large crowds that people were unable to find seating. During the time she spent there, hundreds were saved or healed, and scores received baptism of the Holy Spirit.

6

The Temple
That God Built

Jesus Christ, the Same Yesterday and Today, and Forever.
—Hebrews 13:8, engraved on Foursquare Church

A imee Semple McPherson attacked Los Angeles with a force of physical and mental eagerness and a devout belief that she was following God's call. Her ambitions were great, and the obstacles tremendous. Locally respected pastors had heard of Aimee Semple McPherson and had no desire to share their congregations with her. The city of Los Angeles was overrun with outlandish preachers with names such as "The Cowboy Evangelist," "The Singing Evangelist," "The Gypsy Evangelist," and a mix of others.

Essayist H.L. Mencken described the Los Angeles of the early 1920s:

> The osteopaths, chiropractors and other such quacks had long marked and occupied it. It swarmed with swamis, spiritualists, Christian Scientists, crystal-gazers and the allied necromancers. It offered brilliant pickings for real estate speculators, oil-stock brokers, wire tappers and so on. But the town pastors were not up to its opportunities.[51]

OPENING A LOS ANGELES MINISTRY

Getting ready for opening night at Victoria Hall took a great deal of enthusiasm on Sister Aimee's part and a lot of help from the community. Flowers for the altar were donated. American flags were borrowed. Sister Evelyn Blake, a subscriber to *The Bridal Call*, advanced money for newspaper ads and pale blue drapes to decorate the back of the stage. The small congregation of Pastor Jacobs helped make posters and put up signs in store windows. Sister Aimee wanted an orchestra, too, but Pastor Jacobs declined. He felt musical instruments had no place in church. Having come this far, however, Sister Aimee was not about to be denied. She reminded Jacobs that the Salvation Army was devoutly Christian and used music in its services. She made her point. A Christian orchestra was assembled. The final addition to the revival hall was an outside banner. Eight feet high and fifty feet long, it proclaimed: *Aimee Semple McPherson—Lady Evangelist—Nightly 7:30 P.M. Full Orchestra, Chorus, Holy Ghost Revival!*

Wearing a white nurse's uniform and a dark blue flowing cape, Sister Aimee mounted the lectern and, with outstretched arms, cried, "O *Lord*! We *know* it will take a miracle, and we rejoice and praise Your name even now, for we know it will happen. The seats will be *filled*! The Spirit will *descend*! Souls will be *saved* and *baptized*, the crippled will be *healed*! And this day and the days to come will be recorded with joy eternal in the Book of Life!"[52]

Sister Aimee's sermons stressed the ministry of the soul first, then the ministry of the body. As at all her previous meetings, the sick came to be healed, and apparent miracles began to occur every night. People crowded the hall, and the adjoining rooms, stairways, and even the pastor's office overflowed. Within weeks, the seven-hundred-seat Victoria Hall was too small.

Minnie Kennedy searched for a larger meeting place and found Temple Auditorium, later known as the Philharmonic Auditorium. It seated thirty-five hundred and cost a hundred dollars for three hours of use. In 1919, that was a large sum of money. Sister Aimee prayed and asked the congregation for offerings. Soon, the donations were enough to pay the rent.

The revival concluded at the end of February. That day, four thousand people jammed the hall. By now, the orchestra had been joined by a two-hundred-voice choir.

Aimee McPherson thanked God for all his blessings. She told the audience how grateful she was to those who were filled with the Holy Spirit and attended the services. Her voice was dramatic, her presentation powerful. She told her listeners, "I'm just a little woman, God's handmaiden, the least of all saints."[53] The enthusiastic audience burst out with shouts of glory to God and Sister Aimee.

As a final gesture, Sister Aimee asked God—and her audience—to help find a home for her children. Before leaving the East Coast, she had promised Roberta and Rolf a home of their own. Within minutes, a woman in the congregation had offered land for a house. Then a man offered to dig the cellar, and another volunteered to build the framing, and so on. Aware that her longed-for home was soon to be a reality, after the meeting,

Aimee wrote a column in *The Bridal Call* entitled "The House That God Built." She invited additional contributions. Three months from the date of the issue, her new house had been built and paid for, and Aimee and her family moved in.

Sister Aimee's fledgling congregation was growing, and so was her desire for a permanent facility where she could preach. To build a lasting edifice that would seat five thousand people was a monumental undertaking, especially for a woman evangelist with only voluntary donations to support the construction. As before, her only means of accomplishing great feats was to pray to God and hold more campaigns.

A TRAVELING PREACHER

When her Los Angeles revivals were over, Aimee Semple McPherson began a rigid preaching schedule that her mother had arranged. At each meeting, she made scores of converts and collected thousands of dollars in donations. As she traveled across the United States, she began to write her autobiography.

In early spring 1919, her first stop was San Francisco. Sister Aimee was hosted by Mary and Robert Craig, founders of the Glad Tidings Temple and Bible School. Once again, she packed the church halls.

Many of those who came were Pentecostals; others had read her extensive newspaper advertisements and were simply curious. People came not only to be cleansed in body and spirit, but some also came to be healed. Sister Aimee understood her audience and always insisted upon a ministry for the soul first, then for the body. Even so, healings were a mainstay. After the meetings, a special room was set aside for those wishing to tarry for baptism. Sister Aimee encouraged everyone to be anointed with the Holy Spirit. Those tarrying often spent the entire night praying on their knees.

Robert Craig was eager to have Sister Aimee's support for the Assemblies of God. He encouraged her to apply for official credentials as an evangelist. She accepted his offer and completed the necessary forms, which were rushed to the church's headquarters in Springfield, Missouri. In April, she was officially named an Assemblies of God evangelist. One of the position's perquisites was a 10 percent railroad discount. From San Francisco, Sister Aimee took the train east, stopping for meetings in Tulsa, Chicago, Pennsylvania, and New York City for a city-wide "Holy Ghost Revival."

On an acre of land, she pitched a tent for the month-long revival. Using electric signs, she proclaimed, "Do you want to be Baptised with the Holy Ghost and Fire? Come!" or "Do you want salvation? Come!"[54] Despite the fact that she had chosen a predominantly Catholic neighborhood in the Bronx and the July heat was oppressive, the curious came, Pentecostals came, and the rowdies came. She attributed any local unfriendliness she encountered to Satan and took the opposition as a challenge.

Using *The Bridal Call*, Sister Aimee expressed her most ambitious dream yet. In the February 1919 issue, she wrote an article titled "The Temple." She wrote:

> Of such vast proportions is this temple that there can be no end of the universe where God is to which this great temple does not reach. Of such grandeur is it, this temple with God for its Architect, Christ for its high Priest, made up of living stones composed of blood-washed souls, its domes and arches of divine love and adoration, with saints and teachers for its pillars, and worshippers for its pavement, that it hath no need of height the sun nor the moon to shine on it, for the glory of God doth lighten it, and the lamb is thereof.[55]

Here was the extraordinary vision for the great Angelus Temple that Sister Aimee would successfully build three years later in Los Angeles.

WINNING RECOGNITION AND BREAKING BARRIERS
During 1919, though, Aimee Semple McPherson had other obstacles to conquer. In October, she published *This Is That*, a remarkable autobiography of her early life that chronicled how

God had called the young farm girl to the pulpit and ministry. It contained many of her sermons and writings, as well as photographs and reports of miraculous meetings.

Sister Aimee's next quest was to crisscross United States and hold huge revivals—revivals that would draw public attention and bring recognition for her amazing achievements. Most cities where services were held had civic leaders and pastors representing local churches seated on platforms. Through the pages of newspapers, Aimee Semple McPherson became known for divine healings, in which the faithful walked without crutches, regained lost eyesight, had broken bones healed, or abandoned their wheelchairs. Although her first divine healing had occurred in Corona, New York, two years earlier, it was not until she had won the attention of major city newspapers that people nationwide began to hear about these phenomena. *The Los Angeles Times*, *The Baltimore Sun*, and *The New York Times*, to name just a few, presented her story to millions.

In 1922, Sister Aimee became the first woman to preach a sermon over the radio (a fairly new form of communication). She was so intrigued by the experience that, in 1924, she purchased her own radio station, Kall Four Square Gospel, or KFSG. She was the first woman to have a radio license and operate her own station. KFSG went on the air broadcasting the hymn "Give the Winds a Mighty Voice, Jesus Saves!" Radio station KFSG is now the oldest operating religious station in the nation.

According to a Glendale resident, a typical Sunday sermon began with Sister Aimee entering, dressed as Little Bo Peep in a bonnet and calico country dress and coming down the aisle swinging a tin milk bucket. Attendants carried similar tin buckets. Sister Aimee then noted that the sound of coins dropping in the buckets hurt her ears. The crowd roared with good-natured laughter and the coins were replaced with dollar bills.

With huge, successful revivals, Aimee Semple McPherson traveled as far as Australia. She raised money from donations, from the growing subscription list of *The Bridal Call*, and from newspaper coverage. Everywhere she went, editors and reporters asked for interviews, which she gladly gave. The results were more donations and more subscriptions. Using all these channels, she finally amassed enough money to realize her dream of a temple.

BUILDING ANGELUS TEMPLE

On donated land in Echo Park, California, she built and furnished the 5,300-seat Angelus Temple. The structure had a room that could hold five hundred people set apart from the auditorium for tarrying, awaiting the miraculous gifts of the Holy Spirit that were manifested through prayer or speaking in tongues. Stage curtains flanked a wall painting of the Jordan River looking over a large baptismal pool. Sister Aimee designed the church's enormous stained-glass windows during a trip to Australia. As a final and magnificent tribute to God, a great carving was hung over the stage, proclaiming, "Jesus Christ, the Same Yesterday and Today, and Forever."

Sister Aimee had many gimmicks for raising money. For example, she might stand on a truck bed and sell sacks of cement. She also took in money when Gypsies and members of the Ku Klux Klan bought chairs for the temple auditorium. With donations, campaigns, and volunteered work, the actual cost of the temple remains undetermined—estimates vary from a million dollars to slightly more. By far, the greatest amount she collected at one time was from a Denver revival. There, she "is supposed to have raised $70,000." [56]

Angelus Temple was dedicated on January 1, 1923. The church was filled to capacity three times each day, seven days a week. A fourteen-piece orchestra with a harp, a brass band, and a one-hundred-voice choir played and sang favorite hymns. According to Sister Aimee, in the first six days that the temple was open, eight thousand converts knelt at the altars and fifteen hundred believers were baptized. A thousand young people joined together to serve as the Angelus Temple Foursquare Crusaders.

On the same day of the temple's dedication, Sister Aimee also entered a float in the Pasadena Tournament of Roses parade. The flower-decorated representation of Angelus Temple received the

HOW FOURSQUARE GOT ITS NAME

On a certain day, the heavens suddenly opened and the prophet Ezekiel had a vision from God. According to the Bible, Ezekiel saw a great storm coming from the north, driving before it a huge cloud glowing with fire, with a mass of fire inside that flashed continually. Inside the fire something shined like polished brass. According to the biblical passage: "Behold a stormy wind came out of the north . . . and from the midst of it came the likeness of four living creatures. . . . [T]hey had the form of a man . . . but each had four faces, and each of them had four wings. Their legs were like the sole of a calf's foot, and they sparkled like burnished bronze"(Ezekiel 1:4–8). Beneath each wing were human hands. The four beings were joined wing to wing, and flew straight forward without turning. Each had the face of a man in front, with a lion's face on the right side of the head, the face of an ox on the left side, and the face of an eagle on the back. The symbolism imparted the idea that wherever the spirit went, it would move straight ahead without turning. Sister Aimee equated this concept with the regeneration of Christianity—including the beliefs in the second coming, baptism in the Holy Spirit, and divine healing.

After many sermons based on Ezekiel's visions, Sister Aimee named her religion "Foursquare Gospel." She also composed the first of the Foursquare battle songs. It was used for the dedication service at Angelus Temple:

> Preach the Foursquare Gospel,
> The Foursquare Gospel,
> Clear let the Foursquare message ring:
> Jesus only Savior,
> Baptizer and Healer,
> Jesus the Coming King.*

Today, Foursquare Gospel is international in focus and works to spread the Bible's message of salvation and to reach as many people worldwide as possible. When Sister Aimee died in 1944, there were 410 churches in North America, 200 mission stations, and approximately 29,000 members. Church records today indicate that more than 3.5 million members live in some 123 countries.**

 * Source: Aimee Semple McPherson, *The Story of My Life*. Waco, TX: World Books, 1923, p. 125.

** Source: The International Church of the Foursquare Gospel. Available online at http://www.foursquare.org.

grand marshal award in the annual competition. A month later, the Prayer Tower opened. Men gathered and prayed in two-hour shifts during the night, and women prayed during the day while also answering thousands of requests by mail, telephone, and telegraph. The unveiling of the great pipe organ, with its many stops, chimes, and harps, came on Easter Sunday.

Aimee Semple McPherson was a dramatic evangelist and her church sermons were often stage productions with colorful scenery, a cast of characters, a fascinating biblical story line, background music, and, always, her message of salvation. The temple become a spiritual home for thousands of her followers and provided regular wholesome entertainment for hundreds of neighbors and out-of-town visitors. After she acquired the radio station, her Sunday sermons were broadcast across the entire country.

Sister Aimee Is Kidnapped

If any man wills to be a Christian,
he can be a Christian.
If you go to hell,
you go of your own accord.

—Aimee Semple McPherson

With all the sensationalism surrounding Aimee Semple McPherson's rapid rise to fame and her divine healings, and with her mother controlling the purse strings of the new debt-free Angelus Temple, there was bound to be some discord. Within the congregation, a grievance committee formed and attempted to have Minnie Kennedy ousted. They claimed she was "pernicious, hurtful, antagonistic, unchristian, unjust, and nagging" and said she relied on a "corps of helpers who are of her same temperament . . . ill-bred, uncivil, snappy, overbearing, and unchristian. . . ."[57] The committee threatened that if Aimee did not relieve her mother of her duties, "facts and witnesses are being gathered for the preparation of the action to be filed" with the Los Angeles district attorney's office. In addition, the committee said, the case "would result in 'much notorious publicity and a great hindrance to our work.'"[58]

In her usual manner, Sister Aimee prayed and trusted that God would help her make the right decision. Eventually, the matter ended when the committee was dissolved. Still, petty jealousies and even contempt among some members of the temple did not diminish.

Unwilling to allow difficulties within her ministry to hold her back, she continued with her various pursuits. She wanted her new radio station to be a state-of-the-art operation. To accomplish this, she needed a skilled radio engineer. She hired Kenneth Ormiston, a married man known to have marital problems. As they worked to perfect the station, Sister Aimee saw Ormiston daily, during her evening radio shows and the new morning show, *The Sunshine Hour*. For clarity in broadcasting, Ormiston installed an intercom on her pulpit chair. She would turn it on while the choir sang so he could work on the transmission. Sometimes she laughed and chatted with him while the choir performed. Unfortunately, her voice could be heard in the top balcony. Some people were not pleased and began to suspect that Aimee and Ormiston had more than just a working relationship, even though Sister Aimee made it a point to dine with both him and his wife. Like some of the congregants, Minnie Kennedy also objected to the non-Pentecostal radio engineer, and, eventually, Ormiston resigned.

KIDNAPPED BY THE KLAN

During the 1920s, ugly barriers of racial and ethnic segregation were rampant. Violent intimidation and even murder were not uncommon crimes against African Americans and Mexicans. Sister Aimee attempted to welcome all races and ethnic groups no matter where she appeared. After the main services, she often went to predominantly black parts of town to hold additional prayer meetings. When members of the notorious secret society the Ku Klux Klan showed up at an Oakland meeting, she spoke to them about salvation.[59] After a service at the temple, white hoods and robes were found discarded on the ground in nearby Echo Park.

Some Klansmen had more insidious ideas, however—or so it was reported by the *Denver Post* on June 18, 1922. According to the newspaper account, Sister Aimee was leaving the meeting hall when someone in a car stopped and asked for her prayers. Leaving the building, she passed reporter Frances Wayne and invited her to come along. When they stepped into the vehicle, they were met by two white-robed and hooded Klansmen. The car sped away, and when it finally stopped, the two women were led into a room crowded with Klansmen. The men recited their creed and presented Sister Aimee with a bouquet of white roses, which were meant to represent the purity of her character and morals.

"How many of you are living lives that would stand the full light of day?" Sister Aimee asked.

There was no response.

"So long as you stand for righteousness, and as defenders of the defenseless, I shall pray for you and ask you to pray for me."[60] After she spoke, she and Frances Wayne were driven away and released.

Biographer Edith L. Blumhofer noted:

> Evidence suggests that, while she was in general agreement with some of the Klan's programs—especially their commitment to social purity—she did not share their racist assumptions. Approval of their methods of intimidation likewise seems

out of character for her. But she clearly applauded some of their platform, as did millions of other Americans bewildered by modernity and social change.[61]

Saving the souls of sinners and preaching the Gospel introduced Aimee Semple McPherson to another side of life. Los Angeles and other large cities were home to bootleggers, gamblers, drug addicts, and prostitutes. These people, just like many others, came to the temple—some for divine healing, others to be cleansed of their wrongdoings. In listening to their tearful tales of damaged lives and crushed dreams, Sister Aimee put herself in a seemingly precarious position. These were people who had broken laws and hurt innocent people. As a

KU KLUX KLAN

The Ku Klux Klan has had a long history of violence and hatred, dating back to the aftermath of the Civil War and the Reconstruction era. Freedom for the former slaves represented for many white Southerners a bitter defeat—not only of their armies in the field but of their traditional way of life. White Southerners had to contend with losses of life, property, and—in their eyes—honor. This atmosphere was an ideal place for the Ku Klux Klan to be born.

The Klan originated in Pulaski, Tennessee, with six young men full of ideas for a social club. It would be a secret organization and the officers would have exotic names, such as the Grand Cyclops, head of the group; a Grand Scribe, or secretary; Night Hawks, or messengers; and Lictor, or guard. New members were called Ghouls.

Soon after the club was organized, members began to disguise themselves with sheets and hoods and gallop through the quiet streets of the little town of Pulaski. As news of the group spread, other Southerners formed their own clubs, and mischief quickly turned to violence. Whippings of African Americans came first, but in a few months, there were bloody clashes between Klansmen and blacks, Northerners who came south, and Southern supporters of Reconstruction. The Klan viciously opposed anyone who worked to help blacks make use of their newly won liberty.

Violence escalated and society became generally lawless in areas.

result of her efforts to reach out to those living in the urban underworld, she received mail praising her work—and hate mail also filled her desk drawers. The thugs of the underworld, who had once been ignored by police or paid for protection, were now being taken more seriously, and many leaders of the criminal world were displeased.

CONTROVERSY AND A MUCH-NEEDED REST

In the midst of this volatile situation, Sister Aimee took a room at the Ambassador Hotel. Hounded daily by well-wishers and reporters, conducting dozens of meetings and sermons a week, she desperately needed a rest. In room 330, she found the time to relax and the privacy to work on her sermons and writings.

Congress and the Reconstruction state governments attacked the Klan. By 1868, the group's criminal activities were drawing newspaper headlines. In 1871, Congress passed a tough anti-Klan law and Southerners lost their local jurisdiction over crimes of assault, robbery, and murder. The U.S. president, Ulysses S. Grant, was authorized to declare martial law. Although the violence did die down, a strict system of racial segregation remained in place, and many decades would pass before whites and blacks would share public facilities in the South.

Americans were stunned when the Klan was revived in the 1920s, bringing back a tide of racism, bloodshed, cross burnings, and lynching. During World War I, the Klan took on a new cause—defending the country from foreigners and strike leaders. Now it was not only blacks, but also Jews, Catholics, Asians, immigrants, and bootleggers who were targets for the Klan. In larger cities like Los Angeles, New York, and Chicago, Klan activities were widespread. Newspapers fueled the fires.

When a group of Pennsylvania Klansmen broke away from the central organization, a lawsuit was filed. The Pennsylvania Klansmen fought back, went to court, and exposed the Klan's horrors. Membership dropped and, for a second time, the Klan receded into the background. It has never disappeared entirely, however. It remains in existence—and as racially hostile as ever—today.

A female member of her congregation stayed across the hall. Although this appeared innocent enough, there was questionable gossip. When her mother, Minnie, and others suggested that she needed more rest, Sister Aimee planned a trip to the Holy Land.

Disgruntled church members questioned her use of temple funds. She received a salary of twenty-five dollars a week and had charge accounts in many Los Angeles department stores. The church properties were held in Minnie Kennedy's name. To defend herself, Sister Aimee noted that a donation "is given as a freewill offering of the people, and if they do not want him to spend it in that manner, they should tie a string to it. . . ."[62]

LOS ANGELES 1920, RIFE WITH QUACKS

In describing Los Angeles as it was when Aimee Semple McPherson arrived, author Morrow Mayo wrote:

It is universally recognized that Los Angeles leads the world in the advancement and practice of all the healing sciences, except perhaps medicine and surgery. Eastern medical science having failed either to rejuvenate the members of that multitude of the aged which each year escapes from harsh winter . . . gravitate naturally to the practitioners of divine healing, fortune telling, and miracle-making, all of which are legalized professions in Los Angeles. . . . The city is internationally famous for its metaphysical versatility, and each year erstwhile Christians in alarming numbers desert the orthodox evangelical churches for temples more bizarre. . . . [A]ny soothsayer, holy jumper, herb doctor . . . demonology, join-jerking, witchcraft, spirit-rapping, back-rubbing, physical torture . . . will find assured success and prosperity in Los Angeles. . . . All kinds of quacks . . . the greatest of these, one of the most remarkable women on earth, was, and is, the Reverend Aimee Semple McPherson.*

* Source: Morrow Mayo, "Aimee Semple McPherson," *Los Angeles*. New York: Borzoi Books, 1932, pp. 269–270.

On January 11, 1926, Aimee and Roberta left Los Angeles bound for the Holy Land. Before heading to the Middle East, they first visited Ireland and the parents of Roberta's late father, Robert Semple. Then it was on to London, England, where Sister Aimee first declined to preach, then France, Italy, and Egypt, before arriving in Jerusalem.

At the Wailing Wall, she was surprised to hear the Jews' cry. "It is a plea for the advent of the promised Messiah," a man told her.

"My evangelic spirit almost got the better of me," recalled Sister Aimee. "I could scarcely refrain from disturbing the peace by crying out, He is come! He is come, and shall return again! Where, thought I, on the face of the earth, is there a sight so hopeless, so determined and so pitiful?" [63]

On returning to London, Aimee Semple McPherson accepted an offer to preach in the Royal Albert Hall. On Easter Sunday, she spoke about the second coming of Jesus. The twelve-thousand-seat hall was packed.

After a wonderful vacation and the warm welcome they received in London, Aimee and Roberta returned to Angelus Temple. There, the greatest disaster of Aimee's career occurred. The most damaging newspaper coverage and public scrutiny erupted when she disappeared while swimming at the beach in Ocean Park, California. Suspicions of murder, a romantic affair, and a dubious kidnapping, added to the curiosity over whether she had drowned. The days after her disappearance made sensational front-page headlines in newspapers across the country.

THE KIDNAPPING CONTROVERSY

As Sister Aimee later told her story, on the morning of May 18, 1926, she went shopping in Los Angeles. When she returned home, her mother suggested that she go down to Ocean Park Beach in Santa Monica and relax. Sister Aimee had just finished two long nights of preaching. She invited her secretary, Emma Schaffer, to accompany her. At the beach, she rented an umbrella, put on her green swimsuit, and swam out to the pier. Afterward, she sat down under the shade of the umbrella and worked on the Holy Land slide show she had planned for the following evening. She asked Schaffer, who did not swim, to telephone the temple music director and order two more lantern slides. While Schaffer was gone, Sister Aimee went for another swim. On her return, she was approached by a weeping couple. They said that their baby was dying and asked Sister Aimee to come to their car and pray for the child.

Sister Aimee asked how they had known she was at the beach and they said they had found out by calling Angelus Temple. Aimee was still in her wet bathing suit and declined to go with them. They accused her of wanting to swim rather than save their dying baby. Trusting and sympathetic, Sister Aimee said she would run back and get her robe, then come along. The woman offered her a dark coat, insisting that there was no time to lose. When Sister Aimee reached the car, there was a man at the steering wheel and a woman in the backseat holding what looked like a baby wrapped in a blanket. As soon as she entered the car, Sister Aimee was shoved to the floor and something sticky was pressed to her mouth.

When she awoke,

> A woman was bending over me. I recognized her at once as the same woman who had approached me at the beach. I was lying on an old iron bed, vomiting severely. It was a terrible room. . . . [T]here was only one window, boarded up almost to the top. . . . I imagined we were somewhere near Calexico, as I heard them speak. . . . The only light was from a kerosene lamp.[64]

Sister Aimee was told she was being held for ransom and that the kidnapping had been planned for a long time. The kidnappers did not tell her how much money they were seeking. She pleaded with them, saying that she had to get back to the temple for the Holy Land slide show. Her pleas were ignored. She later said she was gagged and tied at times. She was eventually moved by car to a run-down house in the desert.

At this time, no one knew of her capture and it was believed she had drowned at Ocean Park. Thousands of members of her faithful congregation came to the beach and held prayer vigils. Scores of people reported having seen her disappear, but none of these claims was confirmed. The Coast Guard dragged the waters, looking for her body. Airplanes searched the sea. A glass-bottomed boat peered underwater.

On May 20, *The Los Angeles Times* ran a front-page story, "Faithful Cling to Waning Hope: Men and Women Followers of Mrs. McPherson Grouped on Sands at Venice Pier Praying Their Leader Will Return to Them." According to the newspaper, hundreds waited in a silent mass on the beach. "She can't be dead," the *Times* said. "It is almost a refrain, repeated time and time again, an expression of faith. . . . 'God wouldn't let her die. She was too noble. Her work was too great. Her mission was not ended.' . . . "[65]

Four days later, on May 24, a letter demanding five hundred thousand dollars was mailed from San Francisco and delivered to Angelus Temple. Aimee's mother, Minnie, immediately turned the letter over to the Los Angeles Police Department. For unknown reasons, the letter vanished from the police files. Minnie Kennedy said the money would be raised, and also posted a ten-thousand-dollar reward for her daughter's return, dead or alive.

In the meantime, Sister Aimee told her captors that the church would not be able to raise five hundred thousand dollars and insisted that her people would not pay a ransom. In San Francisco, two men reportedly told police officers that they wanted a blind man to serve as a go-between for Minnie Kennedy and themselves in a ransom meeting. Days later, the ransom price dropped to twenty-five thousand dollars and Minnie Kennedy was asked by police to prepare four questions for the blind lawyer chosen as a go-between to ask her daughter, Aimee—to prove she was still alive.

As the days wore on, Sister Aimee, still held captive in the desert, looked for a way to escape. Tied up and left on a cot, she was sometimes left in the shack alone. She later recalled, "As I lay on the cot, I noticed a tin can on the floor with a jagged lid. It was square like the cans we use for maple sugar in Canada. I rolled off the cot to the floor and managed to squirm to that can. By rubbing the straps and ropes against the jagged edge of the can, and pulling and tugging, I managed to cut them."[66] Once she had broken free, she prayed for God to lead her to safety.

Sister Aimee walked and ran and rested along a deserted road until she came to another shack. The occupant was unshaven and frightening looking, and when she asked if there were any women in the house, he said no. She decided not to go in. A mile or so farther, she met a Mexican couple who gave her some water to drink. She learned that she was across the American border in Agua Prieta, Mexico. Immediately, she asked the couple to find her a taxi. She recrossed the border and went to a police station in Douglas, Arizona. At first, the police did not believe she was the famous evangelist. The editor of the *Douglas Dispatch* was called in to identify her.

When the crowds that were praying at the temple found out that Aimee Semple McPherson was alive, they rushed into the streets, beating drums and blowing whistles, and held a celebration parade. It was June 23. Aimee had been gone for forty-six days.

Sister Aimee Defends Herself

Let her be judged in the only court of her jurisdiction—the court of public opinion.

—Asa Keyes

Aimee Semple McPherson's reappearance was heralded not only by her faithful, waiting congregation but also by the ferocious members of the press. When her identity was confirmed, reporters, photographers, and authorities hounded her. The radio spread the news of her return to the remotest corners. First taken to the hospital in Douglas, Arizona, she was repeatedly questioned by Los Angeles Deputy District Attorney Joseph Ryan and Captain Herman Cline.

After leaving the hospital, she accompanied the policemen to where she thought the shack she had been held in should be. They did not find it. Then the officers took her to a café in Agua Prieta. The leader of the little Mexican village asked to speak to her alone. Through an interpreter, he told her that he had been offered five thousand dollars to say that her story was a lie. He then said that if she paid him what he was being offered by the other party, he would confirm that her account of her escape was true. When she refused to be blackmailed, the man changed his story. Later, however, the interpreter gave a written statement corroborating that the man had solicited a bribe.

INTERROGATIONS AND ACCUSATIONS

The district attorney and police captain accompanied Sister Aimee on her return rail trip to Los Angeles. They questioned her repeatedly, taking breaks during which they went back to the Pullman car and handed newspaper reporters the latest information. At every station at which the train stopped, the media representatives telegraphed their stories to their respective newspapers and magazines.

On the train, both policemen seemed to believe her story. But later, according to Aimee, Ryan called "me a fake and hypocrite."[67] When the Southern Pacific's Golden State Limited arrived in Los Angeles, a crowd of fifty thousand was on hand to meet her. The temple band played and Sister Aimee was carried to a car adorned with flowers. She went directly to the temple and, there, before the altar, she fell to her knees and thanked God for her safe return. More than five thousand people had followed her into the church. The organist filled the auditorium with music of thanksgiving.

When she described her kidnapping and her later escape from her captors, the public's interest in her life intensified. Attempts to analyze and discredit her story filled countless newspaper and magazine pages with bold headlines and banners. Robert ("Fighting Bob") Shuler, head of the Church Federation of Los Angeles and pastor of Trinity Methodist Church, had previously angrily questioned Sister Aimee's unorthodox methods of preaching. After her return, he joined the doubters and sought to destroy her by accusing her of a lapse of morals.

Another so-called eyewitness stepped forward and said that Sister Aimee had been seen at a Dr. Weeks's Douglas office. According to the accusation, the doctor had performed an operation on her, after which she was driven into the desert to recover. The suggestion was that she had had an abortion, which was illegal at that time. Since Sister Aimee had previously undergone a hysterectomy, her medical records proved this claim absurd. Nevertheless, the doctor's secretary was asked to confront her. The secretary replied that she had never seen Sister Aimee before. Dr. Weeks was confronted by a Douglas pastor and he, too, denied

AIMEE'S CRITICS

H.L. Mencken, an American essayist and critic who was known as "the sage of Baltimore," did not restrict himself to literary criticism. He also turned a phrase or two for personalities in fields as diverse as music, language, literature, and religion. He referred to Aimee Semple McPherson as "this commonplace and transparent mountebank." Sister Aimee was also compared with Mary Baker Eddy, who Mencken characterized as "a fraud pure and unadulterated." According to biographer Charles Fecher, Mencken "set forth his frank, unabashed and often outrageous opinions on every aspect of life in America and was the most powerful single force in American criticism in the 1920s."*

* Source: Charles Fecher, *Mencken*. New York: Alfred A. Knopf, 1978.

treating her. Still, the sensationalism surrounding Aimee Semple McPherson would not die down.

As the weeks went on, newspapers explored new ideas for their stories, only to be disproved over the following days. Any and all finger-pointing was spun into a story. *Vanity Fair* magazine had previously run a story called "Vanity Fair's Own Paperdolls," a page of illustrated cutout dolls. The drawings included a caricature of "Aimee McPherson, the wandering evangelist who takes desert hikes, world jaunts and husbands, all in the name of faith." One of the paper doll's outfits was a hard hat underwater diver costume, meant to suggest Sister Aimee's baptismal garb. The doll itself depicted her clad in a pink slip, holding a book, and wearing white kneesocks. All the costumes were adorned with a bouquet of white lilies.

Upton Sinclair, a social reform writer who was later awarded a Pulitzer Prize, wrote a lengthy poem about Aimee Semple McPherson's disappearance called "An Evangelist Drowns." In part it read,

> *My Savior—wilt Thou not save me?*
> *Ten thousand to my aid would run,*
> *Bring me my magic microphone!*
> *Send me an angel, or a boat. . . .*[68]

While writers and artists created more amazing cartoons and stories, Sister Aimee was taken back to Ocean Park. She was asked to show police where the kidnappers had parked their car, and she was shown books with photos of known criminals. Through all the interrogations, the police allowed photographers and reporters to be present. As the press flashed headlines across the nation, Sister Aimee took to the pulpit, where she reminded her followers that the prophet Daniel had been thrown into a den of lions and was miraculously saved, then awarded the highest of honors. Similarly, Nebuchadnezzar captured Shadrach, and with Meshach and Abednego, was cast into a fiery furnace. Because their faith remained firm, they managed to escape unharmed.

SISTER AIMEE GOES TO COURT

With endless rumors, undocumented suspicions, and a rash of claimed sightings, the Los Angeles district attorney finally stepped in. Sister Aimee and her mother were subpoenaed by the grand jury and charged with corruption of public morals, manufacturing evidence, and falsifying police reports. On a hot July 8, Sister Aimee appeared in court. Time after time, she was questioned about every aspect of her captivity, her trek across the desert, and her alleged captors. Jurors doubted that she could survive the desert ordeal without water, without ruining her clothes and shoes, and without suffering more physical injuries. She offered to go back and, without water, walk the escape route again. Her suggestion was refused. She flatly denied having amnesia or creating the kidnapping story to get publicity. Her sanity was questioned.

There were also questions regarding her ministry. Los Angeles District Attorney Asa Keyes wrongfully accused her of having been forced to leave revivals in Denver, Oakland, and Fresno. She was asked about misunderstandings with temple ushers and her secretary, and there were frequent innuendos about her relationship with Kenneth Ormiston. She denied all the allegations.

Minnie Kennedy, Rolf, and some of the temple workers were also interrogated. Even Sister Aimee's hair came under public scrutiny. Some witnesses said she was blond with short hair. Eventually, her attorney asked her to take down her hair. On the witness stand, she uncoiled her thick auburn curls, which fell nearly to her waist. She also retold the story of her life and how God had spoken to her. She swore: "Before the God in Whom I have very faith and utter belief every word I have uttered about my kidnapping and escape is true!"[69]

On July 20, 1926, the grand jury found insufficient evidence to warrant an indictment against Sister Aimee and her mother. Even so, the insatiable press and the sentiment of the public refused to back down. They clamored for more. Three days later, they got what they wanted: There were new revelations. Asa Keyes was tipped off that Sister Aimee had been seen with Kenneth

Ormiston in Carmel-by-the-Sea, a coastal community south of San Francisco, between May 19 and May 29. Allegedly, the two had rented a cottage, and fourteen witnesses identified Ormiston's and Sister Aimee's handwriting on a Carmel grocery slip. (The slips were later lost in the jury room.) Fighting Bob Shuler harangued Sister Aimee from his pulpit, declaring that she was an outrage to Christianity.

To all the outcry, Aimee Semple McPherson responded with a dramatic stage performance at Angelus Temple. *The Devil's Convention*, as she called the show, was set in hell. The auditorium was jammed as Satan and the devils attempted to discredit her testimony. They debated how to destroy Sister Aimee. Satan decided that the best method would be slander. The play ended as two angels descended from the dome of the temple to exonerate her. One carried a sword of truth and the other held a chain to bind Satan and cast him into hell. Sister Aimee cried out, "Oh praise the *Lord*! Forty-six *thousand* new jewels in God's crown! Forty-six *thousand* sinners saved from the clutches of the devil! . . . nine thousand eight hundred and nine *baptized* right here on this platform! Praise *God*!" Her words were lost beneath the thunderous applause.[70]

The battle of words between Aimee Semple McPherson and the authorities, the newspapers, and public opinion continued to rage during the summer months. There were death threats and demands for money. In August, Lorraine Wiseman came to the temple and admitted that she was the one who had been mistaken for Aimee McPherson in Carmel during the supposed tryst with Kenneth Ormiston. More mystery women and dubious men appeared. Sister Aimee fought back using her radio station, and then, *The Los Angeles Times* exposed Wiseman's story as a hoax. The woman was arrested and Aimee Semple McPherson received a demand to pay her bail. When she refused, the woman claimed that she had been hired by Sister Aimee to make up the story.

On November 3, after months of charges and countercharges, Asa Keyes issued a complaint against Sister Aimee, Minnie

AIMEE SEMPLE
McPHERSON

The Salvation Army was founded to help provide services for the needy, as seen in this 1919 advertisement. Although the Army's members were Christians, their unusual worship services often made them controversial. Because Aimee's mother was an avid supporter of the Salvation Army, it played a profound role in her own religious development and her decision to join the Pentecostals—another controversial Christian group.

Minnie E. Kennedy (seen here at right) was a major influence in her daughter's life and work. As a devout Christian, after Aimee began her ministry, Minnie became not only a devoted follower but also a trusted church employee. Although differences later arose over Minnie's management of church affairs, the mother and daughter shared a very close relationship for most of their lives. This photograph of the two of them was taken in May 1929.

It was her desire to build a stable home for her children that helped inspire Aimee Semple McPherson to move to the West Coast, where she founded her permanent church. Seen here in a 1935 photograph with their mother at center are Aimee's children Rolf McPherson (left) and Roberta Semple (right).

SISTER AIMEE SEMPLE McPHERSON

618   ANGELUS TEMPLE. LOS ANGELES, CALIF.

An artistic rendering of the Angelus Temple in Los Angeles, California, depicts the church's founder, Aimee Semple McPherson at top left. Because all of the materials and work for the temple were donated by her spiritual followers, Aimee often referred to Angelus Temple as the church "that God built."

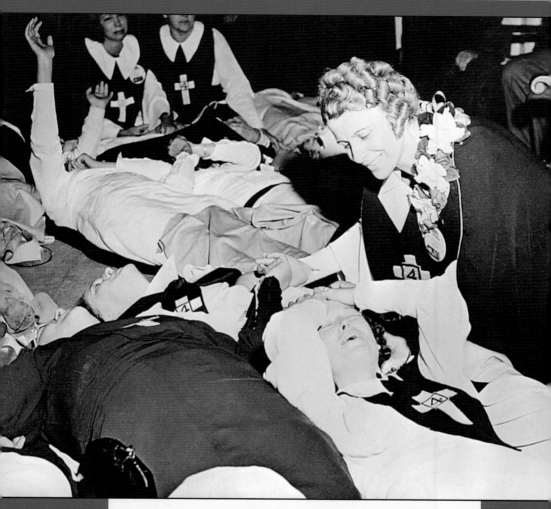

Pentecostals were known for their sometimes strange behavior during worship services, particularly the practice of speaking in tongues in which the believer would be overcome by the power of the Holy Spirit. In this 1942 photograph, Aimee Semple McPherson (right) is seen ministering to members of her congregation who are caught up in a religious fervor.

Aimee Semple McPherson was best known to many Americans for her powerful radio broadcasts. Although Aimee broke barriers with her radio station, it also caused a good deal of controversy in her life. Seen here with radio expert Kenneth Ormiston, Aimee is seated in the radio operating room of Angelus Temple. Because of their close working relationship, some people suspected that Aimee and Ormiston were also involved romantically.

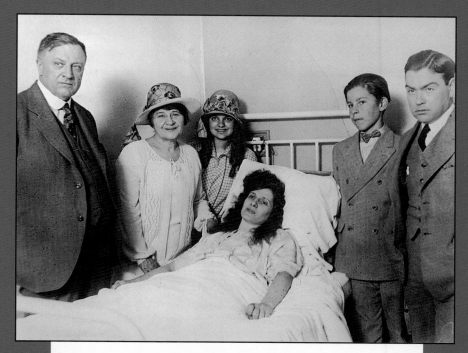

Although it has never been proven exactly what happened to Aimee Semple McPherson during the period she claimed to have been kidnapped, her account of the incident was well documented. Aimee (in bed) is seen here at the hospital, surrounded by investigators and supporters, just after her return from her disappearance.

Aimee Semple McPherson is still remembered for her dramatic performances on stage. In addition to preaching and healing, she frequently wrote and put on pageants and dramas to entertain and educate her followers. She is seen here during a pageant staged as part of a celebration of the twenty-fifth anniversary of her becoming an evangelist.

Kennedy, and another woman on three counts of perjury. The following Sunday, Sister Aimee put on another spectacular drama and sermon, which many people believed was aimed at Robert Shuler. She called it *The Biggest Liar in Los Angeles*. As it turned out, the liar was not Reverend Shuler but the devil—the father of lies.

Testimony on the perjury charges began with questions similar to those the original grand jury had asked. Then a parade of new witnesses, all of whom swore they had seen Aimee Semple McPherson in Carmel, recounted their stories. There were more angry allegations by the district attorney and objections by Aimee's attorney. On October 28, the defense rested its case. Nearly three months later, on January 10, 1927, Asa Keys stated that Aimee Semple McPherson was judged "in the only court of her jurisdiction—the court of public opinion." Upon his request, the case was dismissed.[71]

There were rumors that Keyes had been paid thirty thousand dollars to drop the case. An investigation was started by the Los Angeles county supervisors and Keyes was acquitted. However, he was later found to have accepted other bribes in an oil scandal, and he spent nineteen months in prison at San Quentin. Sister Aimee visited Keyes during his imprisonment.

The truth behind Sister Aimee's kidnapping story remains a mystery today. Her account has never been proven or disproven. Her family and members of the church, however, think the Mafia kidnapped her.[72]

Putting the trial behind her, Sister Aimee made plans for an eighty-day national evangelical tour.

9

The Vindication Tour—and More Controversy

I have perhaps made enemies with such talk, but in everything I have tried to live as a lady and a Christian.

—Aimee Semple McPherson

The Vindication Tour, as its name suggested, took place after the Los Angeles district attorney had cleared Sister Aimee of all charges of wrongdoing. Then perhaps the most famous woman in America, Aimee Semple McPherson may have been hurt and angry because of the drawn-out court trial and the fact that the newspapers and even her public had doubted her story. Even so, she remained a dedicated, God-fearing evangelist.

Minnie Kennedy wanted her daughter to focus on Angelus Temple—to back away from further publicity and keep a low profile until public opinion cooled. Sister Aimee saw the situation differently. She would use all the publicity—the sensational and often erroneous headlines—to help her preach the Gospel and provide themes for her sermons. In the spring of 1927, she set out on a three-month, transcontinental lecture tour.

A NEW APPROACH TO HER MINISTRY

In certain cities, she was a huge success; on other nights, she did not fill the auditoriums. The reason was simple: People had come for the healings and soul-saving she was known for—a glorious revival. Instead, Aimee Semple McPherson lectured about her life, retold the story of her kidnapping and trial, and used her book *The Story of My Life* as an example of her survival.

To help her manage and promote the tour, she hired Ralph Jordan, a former reporter for the *Los Angeles Examiner* newspaper, and his assistant, James Kendrick. Unlike the devout and clean-living temple employees, Jordan was a chain smoker, whiskey drinker, and poker player. But the fast-talking Jordan and Kendrick knew how to handle the press and they proved to be indispensable to Sister Aimee. The rest of her entourage on the tour included ministers, a nurse to help the invalids who sought healings, a choirmaster, her personal secretary, and numerous volunteers from the temple and the local churches where she spoke.

Besides giving her presentations a new format, Sister Aimee had a new look as well. Her long auburn hair was cut and styled in tight wavy curls. She wore makeup and stylish clothes, including tailored suits and chic hats. In New York and other cities (wherever weather permitted), she appeared in a full-length fur coat. No longer riding in her Gospel automobile, she was now chauffeured by limousine. Aimee Semple McPherson was not a movie star, but she was presenting herself as one.

She visited speakeasies, dance halls, and nightclubs. At the Three Hundred Club on West Fifty-fourth Street in New York City, Tex Guinan invited her to speak. Never one to shun the lower classes if she thought she might be able to save souls, she accepted.

"Behind all these beautiful clothes, behind these good times, in the midst of our lovely buildings and shops . . . there is another life," she began. "There is something on the other side. 'What shall it profit a man, if he shall gain the whole world, and lose his own soul?' With all your getting and playing and good times, don't forget you have a Lord. Take Him into your hearts."[73]

Sister Aimee received a standing ovation. The next day, New York newspapers carried glowing accounts of her appearance at the club. *The New Yorker* magazine took a different approach. Paxton Hibben's essay, titled "Aimee and Tex," ridiculed the evangelist with phrases such as "Her legs belong to the school known as piano," and "the middle-aged spread is hidden by the cape she wears."[74] After the thousands of critical words and voices that had been directed against her over the past year, it is easy to assume she was unaffected by Hibben's jibes about the way she looked.

CONTROVERSY CONTINUES

There were more confrontations and criticisms to come, though, after the Vindication Tour was finished and Sister Aimee arrived back at Angelus Temple. First, she had a falling out with her mother. For years, her mother had successfully managed the business side of the church and held the property in her name. She disagreed with her daughter over the tour, however, and about employing Ralph Jordan. She felt that Aimee should be spending more time with her Los Angeles ministry, the Bible school, and the other aspects of the church.

There had been rumblings and meetings about Minnie Kennedy's mismanagement of church affairs. The church board urged Aimee to assume full management of the temple herself. Her mother countered that "unscrupulous schemers were taking advantage at a crucial time." The story, which indicated a rift between mother and daughter, made headlines. In response, Aimee praised her mother: "I have the greatest respect and admiration for her and for all her invaluable services to me over the past many years." Nevertheless, Minnie Kennedy retired. She and her daughter reached an amicable property settlement.[75] Though this crisis was settled in a friendly way, when Minnie Kennedy showed up at a hospital with a broken nose, the press screamed that her daughter had inflicted the wound. Minnie denied the allegation.

THE GROWING CHURCH

While turmoil seemed to hover over Sister Aimee, the temple's work was growing successfully. In 1927, the International Church of the Foursquare Gospel was incorporated. Temple missionaries established churches not only in the United States, but in Latin America, Africa, and Asia. The name of the temple Bible school was changed to LIFE—Lighthouse of International Foursquare Evangelism. Sister Aimee taught five times a week, while also fulfilling her preaching schedule, conducting weddings and funerals, and visiting the sick.

The support and comfort provided by Angelus Temple volunteers and missionaries reached even the areas surrounding Los Angeles. If a family was hungry and called the temple for help, bags of groceries were delivered within hours. Clothing and shoes were given freely to those in need, recalled Nancy Bastajian, who lived up the hill from the Angelus Temple.

In his book *One Man Tango*, actor Anthony Quinn described going to the temple as a young boy. Born and raised a Catholic, he remembered his grandmother being ill and young followers from Angelus Temple coming to pray for her. They invited Quinn to come to their services. "It was nothing like the staid Mass of the Catholic Church," he wrote, "It was bells and whistles, hoots and hollers. A brimstone—but beneath this warm-up act of a sermon there was singing, and laughter, and joyous shouts of Amen! and Hallelujah! and Praise the Lord!" At Angelus Temple, Quinn said he experienced an "epiphany."

He had never seen so many people happy at the same time. Seated in the auditorium, Quinn waited eagerly to see Sister Aimee: "Then the woman on stage spread her arms wide, to hold the silence. The light played off her flowing gown like magic. She riffled the pages of the Bible, and stopped to read where it fell open. When she finally spoke, it was in such a rich melody—Glory! Glory! Glory! that I was lifted and shouted back."[76] Quinn compared Sister Aimee's dramatic performances to the work of the great actresses of the day: "Greta Garbo, Ingrid Bergman, Katherine Hepburn, Anne Magnani— . . . not one of them could touch her."[77]

Sister Aimee and Quinn became friends. He translated and preached for her in the Mexican neighborhoods of East Los Angeles, and he played the saxophone on the street corners to help her gather a crowd. He recalled: "She gave me hope, and confidence, and dignity."[78]

Years later, Quinn was interviewed on television by Edwin Newman, host of NBC's *Speaking Freely*. Asked about Aimee Semple McPherson, Quinn remembered, "All you had to do was pick up the phone and say, 'I'm hungry,' and within an hour there'd be a food basket for you."[79]

NEW ENDEAVORS

Aimee Semple McPherson's book *In the Service of the King* was released in 1928 to cool and volatile reviews. Constance Rourke of the *New York Herald Tribune* wrote: "The book may come as a revelation. The tide of its narration knows only flood. Its sheer emotionalism sweeps one along persistently, even when the conservative reader, to put it mildly, is not entirely in sympathy." [80]

The *New York Times* was even less compromising. Reviewer Herbert Asbury wrote:

AIMEE MEETS CHARLIE CHAPLIN

Hollywood celebrities such as Anthony Quinn, Tallulah Bankhead, and Bea Lillie often sought out Sister Aimee for various reasons. Charlie Chaplin, the so-called King of Comedy, was one who did not. Rather, it was Aimee Semple McPherson who went to see *him*.

In the 1930s, Chaplin, an established producer and actor, was vacationing in France at the same time that Sister Aimee was on a trip to the Holy Land. While in Marseille, she learned that Chaplin was there, too. It had been rumored that Chaplin had come several times incognito to Angelus Temple, and as a result, Sister Aimee was very interested in meeting him. In Los Angeles, such a meeting would have been shocking. But far away from Los Angeles and Angelus Temple, Sister Aimee showed no reservations when she knocked on the door of Chaplin's hotel room.

Chaplin's servant was hesitant, but reluctantly invited her in. When Chaplin entered the room, after his initial surprise, he invited Sister Aimee to dinner. The evangelist and the actor jousted with words.

"I've been to your temple to hear you," Chaplin told her, "and half your success is due to your magnetic appeal, half due to the props and lights. Oh, yes, whether you like it or not, you are an actress.

"Religion—orthodox religion is based upon fear," Chaplin continued, "fear of doing something on earth which will keep them out of heaven. My God, they miss out on all the glorious freedom of life in order to reach a mythical heaven where they can walk on golden streets and play a harp—a bait of pure boredom, it you ask me."

Sister Aimee answered, "Our worlds are different—vastly different."

Despite their differences, they continued their conversation. The next evening, they set out for a long walk around the city. It was later rumored that Chaplin gave Sister Aimee advice about stage arrangements for her illustrated sermons.

Source: Gerith Von Ulm, *Charlie Chaplin, King of Comedy*. Caldwell, ID: Caxton Printers, Ltd., 1940, pp. 330–331.

It is typical tabloid production—a helter-skelter, bubbling, boiling rhapsodic and frequently incoherent mess of religious platitudes often mentioned but is quite overshadowed by the personality of the ballyhooing, go-getting evangelist. . . . Worthless as Mrs. McPherson's book is as literature and as difficult as it is to read, it has a very definite value as a clinical exhibit, and should be tremendously interesting to students of religious psychology.[81]

In the early 1930s, Aimee Semple McPherson began to develop illustrated sermons and sacred operas. These were theatrical productions staged in the temple, with costumes, pastel lighting, painted backgrounds produced by local artists, and music, all geared to convey a message. Sister Aimee herself wrote most of the music and the scripts for *Regem Adorate*, *The Iron Furnace*, *The Rich Man and Lazarus*, as well as songs such as "The Key to Paradise," "The Castle of Broken Dreams," and "Blue Monday." Over the years, these shows brought joy to thousands.

A NEW MARRIAGE AND RENEWED CRITICISM

But with hours of writing, preaching, editing, and producing, Sister Aimee's health weakened and she suffered a near breakdown. To regain her vitality, the following year, she took an ocean voyage. Upon her return home, her workload doubled. She had completed the musical score for her opera *The Crimson Road*, which portrayed the story of the Jews' oppression in Egypt and the ensuing Exodus. The production was planned for Easter Sunday—the only problem was that Sister Aimee needed a singer to play the role of the Egyptian pharaoh. A friend introduced her to David Hutton, Jr. She liked the voice of the short, heavyset singer, and when he proposed marriage, she accepted. To the surprise and consternation of her congregation and the press, they were married on September 13, 1931. To avoid publicity, they flew to Yuma, Arizona, where the Reverend Harriet Jordan, dean of LIFE, performed the wedding ceremony. Almost immediately after the wedding, Sister Aimee was told by a reporter that another woman was preparing to sue Hutton for breach of promise (she claimed he had been engaged to marry her but had broken the engagement). Two days later, the woman filed suit and demanded $200,000. Aimee stood by her new husband's side.

Sister Aimee had always followed the church doctrine that insisted divorced persons should not marry as long as their former partners lived. Yet, during an afternoon service, a senior elder expressed the temple's approval—they accepted her marriage.

Even so, people wondered why she had married Hutton. In her book, she later wrote of her feelings of loneliness and her need for "the protection of a man, the thoughtfulness and tenderness and devotion of a good husband." [82]

After their marriage, Aimee and Hutton flew to Boston to begin a tour there. Her revival started out slowly, not filling the large auditorium. By the last evening of the tour, she drew a crowd of twenty-four thousand. In a single service, two thousand people stood to express their desire to receive Jesus Christ as their savior.

Sister Aimee held more successful revivals before she returned home and then turned around and went out on tour again. This time, she traveled to Central America, where she came down with a tropical fever and was bedridden.

In early July, the case against David Hutton was presented in court. Sister Aimee was in a hospital in Ellsinore recovering. Newspaper headlines raged once again. The personal details about Hutton and the other woman made sensational copy. Sister Aimee remained hopeful that Hutton would be vindicated. After the trial ended, Hutton went directly to his wife. "It isn't bad after all," he reportedly told her. [83] The case was settled for five thousand dollars.

Aimee fainted, hit her head, and suffered a mild concussion.

If that wasn't enough to ruin their marriage, Hutton was also implicated with his friend Roy Watkins in an alleged shakedown of the Angelus Temple commissary. The Los Angeles Social Service

Commission ordered an investigation of the commissary accounts. Supposedly, commissary workers used donated apricots to make brandy, and there were allocations of kickbacks from grocers. Hutton and Watkins denied any wrongdoing. The city briefly suspended the commissary's permit to operate until Watkins was fired.

Despite tremendous pressure to prepare sermons and her dramatic operas, alleged criminal allocations, contract charges, and continuing disputes between Aimee and her mother, Sister Aimee carried on. But by 1932, her health failed again. She announced that she would be leaving the pulpit. She gave power of attorney to Harriet Jordan and then set sail to visit the Foursquare missions scattered around the world. David Hutton remained at Angelus Temple.

10

Triumph
and Tribute

She believed, with all her heart, in goodness and kindness,
and before this fact all else was meaningless.
—Carey McWilliams

S ister Aimee's daily schedule would have overwhelmed today's executives and would have more closely resembled the itinerary of a rock star on tour. Her 1933 whirlwind tour of the United States took place over a period of one hundred fifty days during which she traveled more than fifteen thousand miles. She held revivals in 46 cities in 21 states and broadcast on 45 radio stations with 336 sermons. An estimated one million people heard or saw her live.

WORKING FOR SOCIAL REFORM

This was the era of the Great Depression. Thousands of people were destitute and hungry, and, it would seem, judging by Sister Aimee's success, that they were also starved for the word of God. Across the state of Oklahoma, severe dust storms and drought forced many residents to pack their belongings and head west looking for new opportunities. Families settled in California, and many found religious salvation and support at Angelus Temple.

The temple commissary clothed and fed hundreds of refugees from the Midwest as well as local unemployed residents. Volunteers sewed quilts, children's clothing, and baby layettes. The White Sewing Machine Company of Los Angeles donated machines for the temple's seamstresses to use. Young volunteers visited the newcomers with baskets of food. Sister Aimee persuaded doctors, dentists, and nurses to staff a free clinic. Funds for a soup kitchen were donated by the Yellow Cab Company. During the first month of operation, eighty thousand meals were served. With the gifts came invitations to attend Angelus Temple.

Fighting the ideologies of atheism and communism was another matter. From her pulpit, Sister Aimee not only preached but became a robust conservative debater and proclaimed, "America is not in the market for a red flag [a symbol of communism]." Charles Lee Smith, founder and president of the American Association for the Advancement of Atheism, challenged her to a debate and she accepted.

Smith's platform was, "There Is No God." Sister Aimee countered with, "The World for God."[84] Sister Aimee was the overwhelming winner.

The Foursquare Gospel Church was strongly against the use of alcohol. To emphasize and instill this doctrine, Sister Aimee held a series of public debates on Prohibition, which was the law of the land, since the ratification of the Eighteenth Amendment to the Constitution. She invited movie actor Walter Huston to argue with her. Huston took the opposing side. Once again, Sister Aimee won the debate with the audience's endorsement.

Approval of her married life, on the other hand, did not come as easily. From the beginning, not only the congregation but a wide range of the public wondered why she had married David Hutton, the cabaret singer. By 1933, their marriage had failed and, in February 1934, they were officially divorced.

Sister Aimee continued with her heavy workload, preaching about twenty sermons each week, teaching in the Bible school, and overseeing the many other aspects of her large, thriving church. Her excessive schedule was damaging her life, however. She suffered from "agonizing arthritis . . . insomnia . . . increased dependency upon sedatives to capture the sleep she so desperately needed."[85]

Her declining state of health did not keep her from preaching, producing illustrated sermons and operas, and writing. In 1936, she published *Give Me My Own God*. This book was a stunning account of her travels in the Orient, interviews with Indian resistance leader Mohandas "Mahatma" Gandhi, material she had heard by radio transmission of Italian dictator Benito Mussolini, and personal visits to improbable places such as the floating brothels in China, a harem, and a leper colony.

AIDING THE WAR EFFORT
When the Japanese bombed Pearl Harbor on December 7, 1941, and President Franklin D. Roosevelt asked Congress for

a declaration of war the next day, Sister Aimee accepted the new challenges of patriotism and stood front and center in the war effort. Dressed in red, white, and blue and wearing a garrison hat, she led her brass band and color guard to Pershing Square, Los Angeles. Dozens of American flags fluttered as she held a Victory Bond rally. She prayed for the U.S. troops and asked for the public's support for the war effort. Within just one hour, she sold $150,000 worth of bonds. Two years later, at another rally, she sold another $150,000 in war bonds. According to the International Church of Foursquare Gospel, Sister Aimee sold more war bonds than any other single celebrity.

To inform the public about gas and sugar rationing, air-raid blackouts, and the desperate need to keep blood banks supplied, Sister Aimee turned to her radio station. On weekends, hundreds of military personnel came to Angelus Temple. They were asked to come to the stage, where Sister Aimee presented each of them with a copy of the New Testament and knelt with them in prayer. The Office of War

WITH EYES WIDE OPEN

In the early 1930s, Sister Aimee was invited to speak at a Boston university. She was astonished when the young men who attended belittled God and the Scriptures. "Where is the proof?" they demanded. Sister Aimee accepted their challenge, and set out to look at the world through new eyes. She traveled all over the world, experiencing many cultures and meeting many interesting people. It was upon her return home to the United States, however, that she found her answer to the college men's question.

Enthralled with the visual welcome of the Statue of Liberty, Sister Aimee noticed the inscription on American coins: "In God We Trust!" She wrote: "Let the scornful scoff for the moment, and clouds veil the face of Truth; we are still able to see light through a ladder and to rise up en masse to Praise God!"*

* Source: Aimee Semple McPherson, *Give Me My Own God*. New York: H.C. Kinsey & Company, Inc., 1936, p. 310.

Information and the U.S. Treasury honored her with special citations for her patriotic endeavors, and the army made her an honorary colonel.

During the years the United States fought World War II (1941–1945), Sister Aimee's sermons had a patriotic theme. They included "Foursquare and Uncle Sam," "Remember Pearl Harbor," "Praise the Lord and Pass the Ammunition," to name just a few.

FAREWELL TO THE FAMOUS EVANGELIST

On February 1, 1944, Sister Aimee held a press conference and announced that her son, Rolf McPherson, would be the new vice president of the church. In September, she flew to Oakland to dedicate a new church. She preached on the origins of the Foursquare Gospel and recalled the first vision she had had back home.

The next day, September 27, she planned to preach her classic sermon, *The Story of My Life*. At eleven o'clock that night, she said good night to her son, Rolf.

Sister Aimee was known to take sleeping pills sometimes and that night, evidently unable to fall asleep, she took too many. Near dawn, her heart was racing and she called her doctor in Oakland. He was performing surgery and was unable to take her call. She was referred to another doctor. By then, she had gone into shock. When Rolf came to wake her, he found her unconscious and immediately summoned medical assistance. It was too late. Sister Aimee was dead.

An article in *Time* magazine stated: "After performing an autopsy, three surgeons were unable to agree on the cause of death. Her heart was strong and there was no evidence that she had taken an overdose of the sleeping pills." [86] The possibility of suicide then came into question. A lengthy inquest was held; the jury did not reach its verdict until October 13. The decision ruled out suicide. The coroner then attributed her death to an accidental overdose of sleeping tablets.

Twelve days after Sister Aimee's death, on her birthday, she was laid to rest in Forest Lawn Memorial Park in Los Angeles. Some years before, she had planned her own funeral down to the last detail. It reportedly cost $40,000 and included a large sculptured marble monument that was placed in the park.

Life magazine covered the funeral ceremony and wrote in part:

> Mrs. McPherson's personal history was almost as spectacular as her evangelical craftsmanship. During her careers she figured as a defendant in no less than 45 lawsuits. . . . Her first husband, Robert Semple, an evangelist, died in China. Her second and third marriages . . . ended in divorce. Sister Aimee's troubles did not, however, diminish the ardor of her followers, who trooped by the thousands to her funeral. They sobbed when her son and chosen successor, Rolf McPherson, arose and stood where his mother had so often preached the Foursquare Gospel. "Mother today is not sorrowing," he said tremulously. "She is rejoicing with Our Savior.[87]

The press, which had followed Sister Aimee throughout most of her life, often blasting her with harsh criticism, now praised her and compared her to other renowned religious leaders, such as Martin Luther and Dwight Moody.

A LASTING LEGACY

According to the International Church of the Foursquare Gospel, today there are more than eighteen hundred churches in the United States and nearly thirty thousand churches worldwide. There are currently more than 3.5 million members living in 123 countries around the globe. The church ranks as one of the three or four most distinguished branches of Pentecostalism.

Aimee Semple McPherson had achieved enormous success by following a dream based on a story from the Bible:

And the Day of Pentecost had now arrived. As the believers met together that day, suddenly there was a sound like the roaring of a mighty windstorm in the skies above them and it filled the house where they were meeting. Then, what looked like flames of tongues of fire appeared and settled on their heads. And everyone present was filled with the Holy Spirit and began speaking in languages. They didn't know, for the Holy Spirit gave them this ability (Acts 2:1–4).

CHRONOLOGY & TIMELINE

1890   Born in Salford, Ontario, Canada, on October 9

1896   Enrolled in Dereham Public School

1902   Wins gold medal in public-speaking contest

1905   Enters Ingersol Collegiate Institute (high school)

1906   Publishes letter concerning evolution in
Family Herald and Weekly Star

1907   Meets evangelist Robert Semple

1908   Receives baptism and speaks in tongues in February;
marries Robert Semple on August 12

1890
Born in Ontario,
Canada

1915
Holds first revival meeting

1913
Gives birth to son, Rolf McPherson

1912
Marries Harold McPherson

1875   1900   1915

1908
Baptized with the Holy Spirit;
marries Robert Semple

1910
Goes to Hong Kong as missionary;
Robert Semple dies; gives
birth to daughter, Roberta

1910   Gives first sermon in Victoria and Albert Hall, London, in March; on June 10, arrives with Robert Semple in Hong Kong; on August 17, Robert Semple dies; on September 17, Roberta Star Semple born in Hong Kong; in November, Aimee returns to New York

1912   On February 28, marries Harold McPherson in Chicago

1913   Rolf McPherson born on March 23 in Providence, Rhode Island

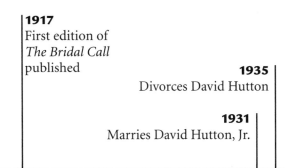

1917
First edition of
The Bridal Call
published

1935
Divorces David Hutton

1931
Marries David Hutton, Jr.

1917   1930   1950

1921
Divorces
Harold McPherson

1923
Starts radio station KFSG

1926
Controversial
kidnapping occurs

1944
Dies in Oakland,
California

1915	Holds first revival meeting in Mount Forest, Ontario
1916–1918	Tours Florida and preaches
1917	Publishes first edition of *The Bridal Call*; preaches in New York and Boston
1918	First transcontinental tour begins in October; on December 23, arrives in Los Angeles
1919	Publishes *This Is That*
1921	San Diego revival held in January; on March 27, ordained by First Baptist Church of San Jose
1923	Radio station KFSG started
1925	Opens LIFE Bible College
1926	On May 18, reported missing after swim at Ocean Park, Santa Monica; on June 23, walks in from desert and tells story of her kidnapping; on September 16, Aimee, Minnie Kennedy, Lorraine Wiseman, and Kenneth Ormiston charged with corruption of morals and obstruction of justice
1927	All charges dismissed; Aimee goes on "Vindication Tour;" publishes *In the Service of the King*; James Kennedy dies on October 20
1928	Tours England
1929	Produces her first opera, *Regem Adorate*
1931	Marries David Hutton, Jr., on September 13; in November, opens soup kitchen
1932	Contracts tropical fever
1933	Produces opera *The Crimson Road*

1935 Divorces David Hutton; makes world tour

1936 Publishes *Give Me My Own God*

1944 Dies in Oakland, California, on September 27

NOTES

CHAPTER 1:
CHINA BOUND

1 Aimee Semple McPherson, *The Story of My Life*. Waco, TX: World Books, 1973, p. 52.

2 Robert Bahr, *Least of All Saints*. Englewood Cliffs, NJ: Prentice Hall, 1979, p. 35.

3 McPherson, p. 51.

4 Bahr, p. 26.

5 McPherson, p. 33.

6 Ibid., p. 38.

7 Ibid., p. 54.

8 Ibid., p. 57.

CHAPTER 2:
GROWING UP

9 Aimee Semple McPherson, *This Is That*. Los Angeles: Foursquare Publications, 1923, p. 16.

10 Ibid., p. 14.

11 Ibid.

12 Charles Darwin, *The Origin of Species*, Chapter 14. Available online at *http://www.literature.org/authors/ darwin-charles/the-origin-of-species/ chapter-14.html*.

13 Robert Bahr, *Least of All Saints*. Englewood Cliffs, NJ: Prentice Hall, 1979, p. 9.

14 Edith L. Blumhofer, *Aimee Semple McPherson*. Grand Rapids, MI: William B. Eerdmans Publishing Company, 1998, p. 56.

15 Daniel Mark Epstein, *Sister Aimee*. New York: Harcourt Brace & Company, 1993, p. 31.

16 Blumhofer, p. 59.

17 Bahr, p.12.

18 Ibid.

19 Ibid., p. 13.

20 Aimee Semple McPherson, *This Is That*, p. 37.

21 Ibid.

22 Aimee Semple McPherson, *The Story of My Life*. Waco, TX: World Books, 1923, p. 28.

CHAPTER 3:
ANOINTED OF
THE HOLY SPIRIT

23 Daniel Mark Epstein, *Sister Aimee*. New York: Harcourt Brace & Company, 1993, p. 50.

24 Ibid.

25 Aimee Semple McPherson, *The Story of My Life*. Waco, TX: World Books, 1973, p. 39.

26 Aimee Semple McPherson, *This Is That*. Los Angeles: Foursquare Publications, 1923, p. 44.

27 Ibid., p. 53.

28 Ibid., p. 55.

29 Edith L. Blumhofer, *Aimee Semple McPherson*. Grand Rapids, MI: William B. Eerdmans Publishing Company, 1998, p. 84.

30 Epstein, p. 69.

31 Ibid., p. 70.

32 National Church of the Foursquare Gospel. "Our Founder." Available online at *http://www.foursquare.org/index.*

33 Barbara A. Campbell, "Aimee: History of Aimee Semple McPherson." Available online at *http://www.members.aol.com.*

34 McPherson, *This Is That*, p. 87.

CHAPTER 4:
CORONA! CORONA!
A HEALING MINISTRY

35 Edith L. Blumhofer, *Aimee Semple McPherson*. Grand Rapids, MI: William B. Eerdmans Publishing Company, 1998, p. 195.

36 Aimee Semple McPherson, *The Story of My Life*. Waco, TX: World Books, 1973, pp. 77, 79.

37 Ibid., p. 78.

38 Daniel Mark Epstein, *Sister Aimee*. New York: Harcourt Brace & Company, 1993, p. 73.

39 Aimee Semple McPherson, *This Is That.* Los Angeles: Foursquare Publications, 1923, p. 90.

40 Epstein, p. 97.

41 Ibid.

42 Ibid., p. 98.

43 Ibid., p. 100.

44 Ibid., p. 101.

45 McPherson, *The Story of My Life*, p. 93.

CHAPTER 5:
SHOUT! FOR THE LORD HAS GIVEN AIMEE THE CITY!

46 Interview with Nancy Bastajian, June 2003.

47 Aimee Semple McPherson, *The Story of My Life.* Waco, TX: World Books, 1973, p. 83.

48 Ibid., p. 96.

49 Aimee Semple McPherson, *This Is That.* Los Angeles: Foursquare Publications, 1923, p. 143.

50 Robert Bahr, *Least of All Saints.* Englewood Cliffs, NJ: Prentice Hall, 1979, pp. 143–144.

CHAPTER 6:
THE TEMPLE THAT GOD BUILT

51 H. L. Mencken, "An Odd Fish," *A Mencken Chrestomathy.* New York: Alfred A Knopf, 1949, p. 292.

52 Robert Bahr, *Least of All Saints.* Englewood Cliffs, NJ: Prentice Hall, 1979, p. 144.

53 Ibid., p. 148.

54 Edith L. Blumhofer, *Aimee Semple McPherson.* Grand Rapids, MI: William D. Eerdmans Publishing Company, 1998, p. 146.

55 Aimee Semple McPherson, "The Temple," *The Bridal Call,* Farmington, MA: Christian Workers Union, Publishers, February 1919, p. 2.

56 Daniel Mark Epstein, *Sister Aimee.* New York: Harcourt Brace & Company, 1993, p. 236.

CHAPTER 7:
SISTER AIMEE IS KIDNAPPED

57 Robert Bahr, *Least of All Saints.* Englewood Cliffs, NJ: Prentice Hall, 1979, p. 174.

58 Ibid.

59 Edith L. Blumhofer, *Aimee Semple McPherson.* Grand Rapids, MI: William D. Eerdmans Publishing Company, 1998, p. 195.

60 Daniel Mark Epstein, *Sister Aimee.* New York: Harcourt Brace & Company, 1998, p. 242.

61 Blumhofer, p. 275.

62 Aimee Semple McPherson, *The Story of My Life.* Waco, TX: World Books, 1923, p. 138.

63 Aimee Semple McPherson, *Give My Own God.* New York: H. C. Kinsey & Company, Inc., 1936, p. 263.

64 Lately Thomas, *The Vanishing Evangelist.* New York: The Viking Press, 1959, p. 63.

65 *Los Angeles Times,* "Faithful Cling to Waning Hope," May 20, 1926.

66 Thomas, pp. 64–65.

CHAPTER 8:
SISTER AIMEE DEFENDS HERSELF

67 Aimee Semple McPherson, *The Story of My Life.* Waco, TX: World Books, 1923, p. 175.

68 Upton Sinclair, "An Evangelist Drowns," 1926. Available online at *http://xroads.virigina.edu.*

69 Lately Thomas, *The Vanishing Evangelist.* New York: The Viking Press, 1959, p. 85.

70 Robert Bahr, *Least of All Saints.* Englewood Cliffs, NJ: Prentice Hall, 1979, p. 232.

71 Thomas, p. 320.

72 Daniel Mark Epstein, *Sister Aimee.* New York: Harcourt Brace & Company, 1998, p. 300.

NOTES

CHAPTER 9:
THE VINDICATION TOUR—AND MORE CONTROVERSY

73 Robert Bahr, *Least of All Saints*. Englewood Cliffs, NJ: Prentice Hall, 1979, pp. 252–253.

74 Daniel Mark Epstein, *Sister Aimee*. New York: Harcourt Brace & Company, 1998, p. 321.

75 Aimee Semple McPherson, *The Story of My Life*. Waco, TX: World Books, 1923, p. 225.

76 Anthony Quinn, *One Man Tango*. New York: HarperCollins Publishers, 1995, p. 66.

77 Ibid., p. 67.

78 Ibid., p. 68.

79 Epstein, p. 380; personal interview.

80 Herbert Asbury, *In the Service of the King*. Book Review Digest, New York: *The New York Times*, February 5, 1928.

81 Constance Rourke, *In the Service of the King*. Book Review Digest, p. 500, New York: *New York Herald Tribune*, April 8, 1928.

82 McPherson, *The Story of My Life*, p. 234.

83 Epstein, p. 374.

CHAPTER 10:
TRIUMPH AND TRIBUTE

84 Edith L. Blumhofer, *Aimee Semple McPherson*. Grand Rapids, MI: William D. Eerdmans Publishing Company, 1998, p. 340.

85 Daniel Mark Epstein, *Sister Aimee*. New York: Harcourt Brace & Company, 1998, p. 435.

86 "Satan at the Seminary," *Time*, October 9, 1944, p. 60.

87 "Aimee Semple McPherson: Thousands Mourn at Famed Evangelist's Funeral," *Life*, October 9, 1944, p. 27.

PRIMARY SOURCES

Book Review Digest. 1928, 1926.

Life magazine. "Aimee Semple McPherson, Thousands Mourn at Famous Evangelists Funeral." October 9, 1944.

Mayo, Morrow. *Los Angeles.* Alfred A. Knopf, 1932.

McPherson, Aimee Semple. *Give Me My Own God.* H. C. Kinsey & Company, Inc., 1936.

———. *The Story of My Life.* World Books, 1973.

———. "The Temple," *The Bridal Call,* February 1919, p. 2.

———. *This Is That.* Foursquare Publications, 1923.

Mencken, H.L. *A Mencken Christomathy.* Alfred A. Knopf, 1949.

Quinn, Anthony. *One Man Tango.* HarperCollins, 1995.

Time. "Satan at the Seminary." October 9, 1944.

Vanity Fair. "An Evangelist Drowns." 1926.

———. "Cut Out Dolls From Vanity Fair." 1920.

SECONDARY SOURCES

Bahr, Robert. *Least of All Saints.* Prentice Hall Inc., 1979.

Bishop, Peter, and Michael Darton. "The Pentecostal Churches." *The Encyclopedia of World Faiths, An Illustrated Survey of the World Living Religions.* Facts on File Publications, 1995.

Blumhofer, Edith L. *Aimee McPherson: Everybody's Sister.* William B. Eerdmans Publishing Company, 1993.

Epstein, Daniel Mark. *Sister Aimee.* Harcourt Brace & Company, 1993.

Fecher, Charles A. *Mencken: A Study of His Thoughts.* Alfred A. Knopf, 1978.

BIBLIOGRAPHY

"Pentecostal." *Webster's New Edition Encyclopedia*. Prentice Hall, 1990.

Southern Poverty Law Center. *A Hundred Years of Terror*. 2000.

Thomas, Lately. *The Vanishing Evangelist*. The Viking Press, 1959.

Von Ulm, Gerith. *Charlie Chaplin King of Tragedy*. The Caxton Printers, Ltd., 1940.

WEBSITES

Campbell, Barbara A. "A Brief History of Aimee Semple McPherson," Aimee Semple McPherson Resource Center (April 2003)
http://www.members.aol.com

International Church of the Foursquare Gospel. "Group Profile." (May 2003)
http://www.foursquare.org

———. "Our Founder." (May, 2003)
http://www.foursquare.org

Salvation Army Collectibles. "General Evangeline Booth." Salvation Army's National and International Websites. (June 2003)
http://www.sacollectables.com

———. "William Booth, A Brief History." Salvation Army's National and International Websites. (June 2003)
http://www.sacollectables.com

Stanford Education Group. "Influenza Pandemic of 1918." (June 2003)
http://www.stanford.edu/group/virus/uda/

———. "The Medical and Scientific Conceptions of Influenza." (June 2003)
http://www.stanford.edu/group/virus/uda/

INTERVIEWS

Bastajian, Nancy Donato. La Crescenta, California. March 2003.

Yarbrough, Charles. Glendale, California. 1940.

PRIMARY SOURCES

McPherson, Aimee Semple. *Give Me My Own God*. H. C. Kinsey & Company, Inc., 1936.

———. *The Story of My Life*. World Books, 1973.

———. "The Temple," *The Bridal Call*, February 1919.

———. *This Is That*. Foursquare Publications, 1923.

Quinn, Anthony. *One Man Tango*. HarperCollins, 1995.

SECONDARY SOURCES

Bahr, Robert. *Least of All Saints*. Prentice Hall Inc., 1979.

Blumhofer, Edith L. *Aimee McPherson: Everybody's Sister*. William B. Eerdmans Publishing Company, 1993.

Clare, John D. *First World War*. Harcourt Brace & Company, 1994.

Collins, David R. *Woodrow Wilson: 28th President of the United States*. Garrett Educational Corporation, 1989.

Epstein, Daniel Mark. *Sister Aimee*. Harcourt Brace & Company, 1993.

Paulsen, Gary. *The Tent: A Parable in One Sitting*. Harcourt Brace & Company, 1995.

Thomas, Lately. *The Vanishing Evangelist*. The Viking Press, 1959.

Tyler, Parker. *Chaplin: Last of the Clowns*. Horizon Press, 1972.

Wellman, Sam. *Billy Graham: The Great Evangelist*. Chelsea House Publishers, 2001.

Zeinert, Karen. *The Extraordinary Women of World War One*. Millbrook Press Inc., 2002.

FURTHER READING

WEBSITES

Aimee Semple McPherson
http://www.aimeesemplemcpherson.org/bio.php
Provides information about Aimee Semple
McPherson's life and ministry.

Aimee Semple McPherson
http://www.geocities.com/wavesofglory/aimeemcpherson.html
An admiring account of McPherson's life and work.

Aimee Semple McPherson
http://www.kamglobal.org/AimeeSempleMcPherson/
mcphersondirectory.html
Provides a chronological view of Aimee Semple McPherson's life,
along with a listing of healings she performed.

Aimee Semple McPherson, Foursquare Gospel Church
http://www.ondoctrine.com/10mcpher.htm
Includes biographical information as well as an overview of the
doctrine of the Foursquare Gospel Church, which Aimee Semple
McPherson founded.

Creative Quotations from Aimee Semple McPherson
http://www.creativequotations.com/one/1456.htm
A collection of sayings by the famous evangelist, along with links
to books and other resources about her.

Destiny Foursquare Church
http://www.destiny4square.org/
An evangelical site that includes essays and other information
relating to Aimee Semple McPherson.

International Church of the Foursquare Gospel
http://www.foursquare.org
The official site of the international church founded by Aimee
Semple McPherson.

INDEX

INDEX

page:

B: Courtesy of the Library of
Congress, LC-USZC4-10026

C: © Bettmann/CORBIS

D1: © Bettmann/CORBIS

D2: © Rykoff Collection/CORBIS

E: © Bettmann/CORBIS

F: © Bettmann/CORBIS

G: © Bettmann/CORBIS

H: © Bettmann/CORBIS

Cover: Associated Press, AP

ABOUT THE CONTRIBUTORS

SILVIA ANNE SHEAFER is the author of fifteen nonfiction books and the recipient of numerous journalism and photograph awards from the California Press Women, Whittier Writer's Club, and a young adult book-of-the-year (1997) from the New York Public Library. Currently, she teaches creative writing at two California colleges and a writing enrichment program for children—College For Kids. She resides in Carlsbad, California.

MARTIN E. MARTY is an ordained minister in the Evangelical Lutheran Church and the Fairfax M. Cone Distinguished Service Professor Emeritus at the University of Chicago Divinity School, where he taught for thirty-five years. Marty has served as president of the American Academy of Religion, the American Society of Church History, and the American Catholic Historical Association, and was also a member of two U.S. presidential commissions. He is currently Senior Regent at St. Olaf College in North-field, Minnesota. Marty has written more than fifty books, including the three-volume *Modern American Religion* (University of Chicago Press). His book *Righteous Empire* was a recipient of the National Book Award.